Harboring the Spirit of Jezebel

"Caught in the web of Destruction"

By: Robert Summers

**Published by
Summers Ministries
Columbus, Ohio**

Harboring the Spirit of Jezebel
Copyright © 2014 by Apostle Robert Summers
All rights reserved

No part of this book may be reproduced, stored in a retrieval system, or transcribed in any for or by any means, electronic or mechanical, including photocopying and recording, without prior written permission of Apostle Robert Summers, Sr. or Summers Ministries.

Cover Design by: Smith Graphic Design
in coordination with CI-Media

Printed in USA by 48HrBooks

Dedication

This book is dedicated to my son David Summers, USMC.

How can peace exist as long as the fornications of your mother Jezebel and her witchcrafts are so many?

2 Kings 9:22(b) Amplified Version

Table of Contents

Introduction
Chapter One ………….. Prime Targets
Chapter Two ………….. Prime Suspects
Chapter Three ………… Harboring the Fugitive
Chapter Four ………….. Aftershock
Chapter Five ………….. Deliverance Prayers

Introduction

The intensity and magnitude of spiritual warfare against the Kingdom of darkness has escalated to perhaps unprecedented levels over the past twenty years. Out of the dark underworld, an ancient evil spirit has come to the forefront that masquerades as a Servant of God. This should be no surprise considering Satan himself can masquerade as an Angel of Light.

And no marvel; for Satan himself is transformed into an angel of light. Therefore it is no great thing if his ministers also be transformed as the ministers of righteousness; whose end shall be according to their works – 2 Corinthians 11:14-15 (KJV)

The name of this counterfeit is *Jezebel*. She calls herself a prophetess but is nothing more than a witch that lures the saints of God away from righteousness and true holiness.

Some of the greatest and most devastating attacks against churches, ministries and families, originate from the Jezebel spirit.

Over the years there has been much teaching on the topic of Jezebel. Many fine authors and deliverance ministers have contributed in providing the body of Christ with a substantial collection of books, CD's and educational materials regarding this ancient evil spirit's history; it's operation and manifestation.

The purpose of this writing is to provide leadership and their flock with an additional resource, one that addresses the infiltration of the spirit of Jezebel and her network in the lives of believers and churches.

Most people look to identify this spirit operating in others. But how does one determine when they are the one being used by this demonic warlord? Further, we need to understand the affects that Jezebel, together with her web and her eunuch's has on those that become targets of assassination.

Jezebel's web of seduction is extensive, and penetrates into places that many have difficulty identifying as a derivative of her operation. I have found that this spirit is capable of camouflaging itself in a manner that will have you looking in another direction. Worse yet is Jezebel's cunning craftiness to potentially seduce leaders and peers into supporting her network. Jezebel works hard to gravitate people into her network and create a point of agreement.

No one is exempt from the diabolical plots, trickery and deception of Jezebel. Through successful seduction of King Ahab, Jezebel perverted and led the nation of Israel into Baal worship (1 Kings 16:31). The ultimate goal of the Spirit of Jezebel is destruction. The Jezebel spirit is born out of witchcraft and idolatry and is intended to destroy the host (the person that the spirit is operating in and through), children, families, relationships, marriages, friendships, churches, prophets, prophetic operations, apostolic authority and the body of Christ at large. Jezebel extends mercy to no one.

This spirit existed long before Jezebel was born. Jezebel is a spirit without gender, working in both males and females. The spirit of Jezebel is an enemy of the Kingdom of God. She defies the very government of God and resists all authorities. The Kingdom of God opposes the spirit of Jezebel.

The name "Jezebel" literally means "without cohabitation," for she refuses to cohabit with anyone unless she can manipulate, control and dominate the individual in a relationship.

Jezebel has absolutely no regard for Godly authority and operates in complete opposition to the will of God with the intent of stopping His plans.

Because the Kingdom of God is governmental in nature, it demands Jezebel to be dethroned from the seat of authority.

When the spirit of Jezebel manifests or is identified by anyone in the church, there should immediately be a surge of deliverance, spiritual warfare and bold preaching of the Word of God. However, much more is needed, not only to root Jezebel out, but also dismantle her controlling network and destroy her eunuch's. It is critical that the church or ministry is properly prepared to engage in battle. This will require communication, exposure and a strategy to keep collateral damage at a minimum.

Since the spirit of Jezebel operates in people, there may be some resistance by peers and church members to address this. They have good intentions and desire that things work in a peaceful manner. They will be prone to wanting to address this situation diplomatically and pass the situation off as simply a "point of prayer." This position must be avoided at all cost.

Leaders, teams, individuals, families and spouses cannot harbor the fugitive called Jezebel. To harbor means to protect, provide a safe haven, shelter, conceal, embrace and entertain.

I believe many saints are unknowingly harboring the spirit of Jezebel in our churches, ministries, families and businesses. Some people form an association, alliance and confederacy with her in the form of friendships and peer groups.

Churches will never develop cutting edge ministry or flourish while harboring a person with a Jezebel spirit. The Jezebel spirit is gruesome and seeks to destroy anyone with a position of authority. Apostles, Prophets, Pastors, church administrators, intercessors, worship leaders, and media staff are all likely targets for her to cause confusion and usurp authority.

Jezebel is a murdering spirit who is *"drunk with the blood of the saints"* (Rev. 17:6)

Jezebel stirs up strife and confusion in churches, families and businesses.

But there was none like unto Ahab, which did sell himself to work wickedness in the sight of the Lord, whom Jezebel his wife stirred up – I Kings 21:25 (KJV)

God speaks expressly against this ancient evil spirit and demands set-leaders to eradicate the spirit from the churches.

Notwithstanding I have a few things against thee, because thou sufferest that woman Jezebel, which calleth herself a prophetess, to teach and to seduce my servants to commit fornication, and to eat things sacrificed unto idols – Revelation 2:20 (KJV)

I have found that the spirit of Jezebel is assigned to churches. She is sent to stop the spirit of God from operating in the lives of believers. Jezebel desires to control the praise and worship, pervert the prophetic, extinguish prayer and ultimately kill the visionary. She is the mastermind of dysfunction, confusion, scandal and division.

Over the years I have battled this ancient sprit numerous times. Jezebel is relentless. She typically manifests when shifts, upgrades and promotions are occurring. Her goal is to stop what God is doing by frustrating leaders and accusing the brethren to each other.

Because Jezebel is a spirit, we must contend with her in the spirit. We are not fighting flesh and blood but principalities and demonic hosts in the unseen realm.

For we wrestle not against flesh and blood, but against principalities, against powers, against the rulers of the darkness of this world, against spiritual wickedness in high places – Ephesians 6:12 (KJV)

Indiscriminately calling or implying that someone is harboring a Jezebel spirit is not only irresponsible but it can be very hurtful to a person. Deliverance and freedom is the ultimate goal. Love must be at the center of everything we do. The word of God instructs us to restore our brother and sister, not beat them up by hurling accusations at them.

Brethren, if a man be overtaken in a fault, ye which are spiritual, restore such an one in the spirit of meekness; considering thyself, lest thou also be tempted – Galatians 6:1

The goal of every quality deliverance minister is to liberate believers from the strongholds that exist in their soul so that they can be productive citizens in the Kingdom of God. They understand that the enemy is not the person that is demonically bound, but rather the demons and evil spirits. However, there is a natural realm application to this spiritual war.

Most believers are not sufficiently equipped to address the spirit of Jezebel because they are unable to apply spiritual warfare to everyday life. They have a propensity to separate the seen and unseen realm rather than operate simultaneously in both realms. Breakthrough believers must not only understand spiritual operations, but also the natural administration of this warfare.

Jezebel walks among us. She is in our meetings, sits next to us in Sunday's church service and can even be a prayer partner. How does one behave when this spirit is in operation in the people that we genuinely love?

This book is designed to assist leaders, deliverance ministers and believers in:

1) Identifying, isolating and eradicating the spirit of Jezebel from their church or ministry in a practical and effective manner.

2) Diagnosing the possibility of being a sympathizer (harboring) to Jezebel

3) Manage the aftershock of Jezebel's departure

4) Receive deliverance and healing from Jezebel and Ahab spirits.

5) Receive a better understanding on how to address the person hosting the spirit of Jezebel.

The topic of Jezebel is so vast that it demands volumes to be written about it. This book is simply scratching the surface *per se*, and is not designed to address all aspects of the spirit of Jezebel or her network. However, it will provide the reader with some present-day truth into Jezebel's operation and controlling network. Finally this book will assist the reader in how to engage the human factor (the person) in a manner that minimizes the casualties of war.

Chapter One

Prime Targets

The Jezebel spirit is born out of witchcraft and rebellion. This demon is one of the most common spirits operating in the church today. She preys on sincere believers whose hearts are for God and on leaders that have passion for ministry.

Jezebel is a spirit and as such, is gender neutral. We refer to Jezebel as a "she", simply due to the fact that this spirit operated in an actual Queen that lived thousands of years ago. Her name was Jezebel. However, Jezebel targets both males and females, although women appear to be more susceptible to her first strike and then potentially used as a host. Men on the other hand appear to be victimized more by Jezebels attacks than to operate as a host. Regardless of being a host or a victim, Jezebel's masquerade of trickery, sorcery and seduction targets a vast array of people and groups.

As any demon, the spirit of Jezebel gains access into one's life by way of sin. Sin opens the door and provides the point of access necessary for Jezebel to attack. Anger, jealousy, hatred, rage or any other thought and emotion that remain unchecked are dangerous things. In the book of Genesis we find that Cain was jealous over God's acceptance of Abel's offering but not his. The spirit of Jezebel will crouch at the door of sin waiting for an opening to come in and weave her web of destruction.

And the Lord said to Cain, Why are you angry? And why do you look sad and depressed and dejected? If you do well, will you not be accepted? And if you do not do well, sin crouches at your door; its desire is for you, but you must master it – Genesis 4:6-7 9 (Amplified bible)

Watch for this spirit to target men and women who are embittered against authority, either through neglect, misuse, or abuse of authority. The Jezebel spirit manifests itself by attacking God's original creation and plan; specifically the relationship He has with mankind and the roles of men and woman on the earth.

Men

Men in general are targets of Jezebel. However, passive men that will not confront issues or embrace their responsibility to lead, fits nicely into Jezebel's plot to overthrow all authorities and take control of churches and families. In deliverance ministry, this type of man is commonly referred to as an "Ahab."

Ahab type men are extremely selfish and they are typically more concerned with spending time in their "man cave" than the things of God. They are consumed by the desire to be successful and must have their way all the time. They are "girly men" in the spirit and prime targets for Jezebel to seduce them emotionally, sexually and spiritually.

Jezebel hates men and is determined to destroy them. She is unable have a true Godly relationship with men. She looks to emasculate them and undermined all authority that they have, whether in the family, business or church.

Jezebel looks to remove fathers from the home. She will use seduction, perversion and pornography as tools to get a man to engage in an adulterous affair or inappropriate text messages, chat rooms and late night Internet porn sites. Jezebel's seducing power over men is often in the form of flattery. Pastors, husbands and males in key positions of leadership are likely targets of this seduction.

The female host of Jezebel will flatter powerful men with attention and look to establish a stronghold that provides her with easy access for "on-demand" conversations.

In the home, Jezebel looks to "wear the pants" and desires to be the controlling boss. The spirit of Jezebel will incite a wife to publicly humiliate her husband with her sharp tongue to show who's in charge. Jezebelic women are often seen as overbearing, bossy, in-control, extremely talkative (to the point of talking over their husband) and dominating.

Additionally, Jezebel will use children as instruments of control and manipulation to advance her agenda. Watch for women that do not permit male children to mature into independent men. Mother's that continue to care for their grown sons well into their twenties, thirties and beyond, create friction in the home. This is a strategy deployed by Jezebel to frustrate the husband and weaken the role of men in the home. Jezebel has a powerful demonic ability to intimidate and irritate, ultimately causing many men to withdraw and give up.

Jezebel is a militant dictator in the home and seeks to destroy the functionality of the family to ensure that her husband and her children will not be able to operate independent of her. Her ultimate goal is to remove the man from the home via separation or divorce.

Women

Although the spirit of Jezebel is genderless, women are sought out due to their unique ability to manipulate with emotions, seduction and body language.

Prime targets are women that have experienced abuse from their father, former spouse or lover.

Additionally, look for Jezebel to target women who are bitter because their biological father abandoned them at an early age. Young girls that did not have any father in the home or no relationship with their father can feel as if they were robbed of the entitlement. Indeed no one can deny the pain of not experiencing the love, happiness and safety of a father-daughter relationship. Nonetheless, Jezebel will exploit any weakness in a person's life and probe into the deep wounds of rejection to determine the best strategy to utilize this victim for her network.

Divorced women are also targets. Divorce is an ugly monster that brings much pain to all parties involved. The Jezebel spirit is a covenant breaking spirit that destroys marriages. Children and both spouses can become scarred for life from divorce. Deliverance and healing is needed for everyone involved. Any un-forgiveness or bitterness will quickly become points of access for Jezebel. Divorce can bring shame, embarrassment, guilt, hurt and rejection. If left unresolved, anger, rage and hatred can enter in. Watch for Jezebel to connect divorced women with others that have experienced the pain of divorce or hurt from men.

Women that have been tricked by men into sleeping with them through the promise of marriage or false words of love can become hurt and angry. Repeated events or conversations with other women that have experienced similar situations can quickly shift the woman's mindset into one that views all men as "dogs." Jezebel will capitalize on this opportunity and look to develop a stronghold in the person's life.

One of the tactics of Jezebel is to lead hurt and abused women down a dark path of homosexuality. Jezebel's perversions include lesbianism. She will link others that have experienced male abandonment and get them to engaged in sexual acts of worship to the ancient gods of homosexuality.

Finally, women that have been hurt by Pastors and church leaders are targeted. Jezebel will employ demons of retaliation that will have easy access to the host holding on to past hurt, shame and pain. Anger and hatred will drive the host to a place where Jezebel can release a fury of vengeance against the Pastor.

Hurt, wounded and abused

Jezebel targets deeply wounded people with emotional hurts to manipulate and control them into doing her bidding. Individuals with a history of emotional and physical abuses are prime targets to be assimilated into Jezebel's Network.

Many people have become wounded through words.

Negative and harmful words spoken by those that normally should reflect love, support and encouragement can have adverse effects on people's lives.

Demonic spirits always look to torment children at very young ages with various degrees and methods of abuse. Parents have a responsibility to nurture their children with love, protection and care. When this fundamental responsibility is neglected or breaks down, it opens a door for the spirit of rejection to come in.

Even while a child is in the womb, words released have a great impact. Spirits of rejection will enter into a child's life even prior to birth due to negative, evil and hurtful words. An unwanted child will experience various levels of the manifestation of rejection demons. Later on in life, the now grown individual carries the past with them everywhere they go.

Young children that experience hostile and traumatic events such as verbal, physical or sexual abuse will be traumatized by demons.

This holds true for adults also, especially married couples. Physical abuses by parents, spouses, relatives and authoritative figures through beatings, tortures and afflicting wounds are all portholes for entrance of rejection demons. Those that have experienced abusive adult relationships may find themselves as recruits for Jezebel's rebellious network. Jezebel is consistent in her pursuit for wounded people that can join into to her web of destruction.

Additionally, males and females alike that have been abandoned by their natural biological father are prone to rejection. Jezebel will summon and deploy demons of insecurity, lust, guilt and shame to develop a stronghold of rejection.

I believe rejection is the strongman that prepares the way for the diabolical spirit of Jezebel to maneuver within a host.

There are many causes for rejection to enter into one's life. Of course, not all rejection is the same. For example, the fear of rejection is the pain of being rejected by others and the strong need for love that has gone unfulfilled by those whom it was needed from, such as, parents, siblings or a spouse.

On the other hand, self-rejection occurs when one thinks that the reason people don't love them is because of something they've done. They believe that they are the reason people abused them and if they "do something", they will be loved.

Individuals that have been bound by a spirit of rejection will look to compensate for the pain and torment of rejection. Rebellion is a common response to rejection. Internal anger manifests in the form of rebellion against those groups, classes or races of people that have harmed the person.

For rebellion is as the sin of witchcraft, and stubbornness is as iniquity and idolatry – I Samuel 15:23 (KJV)

Rebellious people are susceptible to hosting the sprit of Jezebel. Rebellion is witchcraft and Jezebel was birthed out of witchcraft. Rebellion creates the perfect environment for Jezebel to release her whoredoms and witchcrafts.

And it came to pass, when Joram saw Jehu, that he said, Is it peace, Jehu? And he answered, What peace, so long as the whoredoms of thy mother Jezebel and her witchcrafts are so many – II Kings 9:22 (KJV)

Jezebel is a sympathizer and will gravitate to those that have been wounded. She will look to create deep soul ties with "'victims" of abuse. Jezebel will take on the role of a mother. False mothering is one the manifestations of a Queen Jezebel. A queen Jezebel is the chief demon that establishes dominance among other Jezebels or eunuchs. Jezebel attracts people to herself through false compassion and pity. Her objective is to lure people away from genuine apostolic fathers, family members and friends and those who can truly speak into their lives.

Jezebel will show signs of concern and motherly nurturing to those she is targeting as her children. She will look to display this behavior in front of others so that if she is ever identified and challenged she has a group of sympathizers and witnesses that can attest to her "genuine love for others". This is purely a show and a performance to cover up her network of perversion.

Jezebel will ask questions such as "is everything alright" or, "are you okay"? Be careful! Jezebel is probing for information so she can draw you into her web.

She will make statements like "I understand what you've been through in life and I'm here to share in your pain". Or her classic statement, "I'm with you and got you covered". These are Jezebel's deliberate acts or trickery and sorcery intended to create a false security in her compassion.

Jezebel will probe your life to identify any insecurities, inferiorities or phobias you have. She will put forth intense effort to cultivate a sense of security through flattery and false commitment. Her desire is to appeal to the flesh and act as if she is different from others and will never leave you. Her goal is to enter in to a soul tie with her recruits.

Un-forgiveness & Bitterness

Because of past hurts, abuses, betrayal and offense many individuals become unwilling to forgive those that hurt them. Over time, roots of bitterness can extend deep into the soul of a person. Jezebel spirits capitalize on and feed off of un-forgiveness and bitterness. They become fuel for her fire. Un-forgiveness is a magnet that draws the Jezebel spirit. A heart that is full of hurts and wounds is fertile ground for Jezebel to plant her seeds of destruction.

Past hurts must be forgotten. Constantly recalling past memories that have never healed results in un-forgiveness. This un-forgiveness subconsciously motivates every decision made regarding relationships and spiritual growth. Jezebel will plant seeds of suspicion towards everyone that resembles those that hurt, abused, betrayed or offended him or her from a previous time.

Forgiveness must be extended not only to those that hurt you, but also to oneself. Satan is the accuser of the brethren and is a liar. One of his strategies is to have believers carry heavy weights of guilt and shame. Un-forgiveness to self is another inroad for the spirit of Jezebel.

Those that are bound by the stronghold of rejection will display patterns and behaviors that are self-abusive. One of the ways that this will manifest is through self-accusation. The rejected person looks to tear down his/her own self-worth. Un-forgiveness of oneself will have a person think that everything is their fault, or the reason they were abused is due to something they did.

Pastors & Leaders

Leaders are one of Jezebel's prime targets because she needs control and influence to extend her network. Jezebel delights in having power.

The Jezebel spirit will use the element of surprise to control and manipulate her victim. The Jezebel spirit will catch you off guard and show up when you least expect it. Pastors and ministers are usually approached immediately after they have released powerful words and are "open" to her strategies. I've had numerous times where this spirit has attacked me after preaching, teaching, prophesying or praying for people. It will meet you as you walk off the platform, down the hall or into your office. Jezebel will say something like, "Apostle, I wanted to share something with you," or, "do you have a minute?"

Be careful of who prays for you. Jezebel is famous for releasing word curses over leaders through prayers of witchcraft. Never permit people to lay hands on you after preaching the word of God.

Jezebel will twist and turn information that Pastors provide, either from the pulpit or in meetings. She is a master at lying, pouting and crying. She will do anything to make a Pastor appear to be in error, unloving, out of order and unstable. Her goal is to bring confusion and chaos to churches and ministries.

Jezebel desires a close personal relationship with the set-leader of the ministry. She can become very controlling and will text, email or call at various points during the day. Men must be aware of Jezebel's cunning craftiness and flirtatious words of seduction.

The spirit of Jezebel forms religious relationships and alliances with multiple ministries, churches and networks in order to obtain information that can be used to undermine leadership. As these relationships are formed, she will plot to instigate jealousy, envy and discord between leaders.

Jezebel loves to take pictures with Pastors and leaders. Hosts that have been intoxicated by Jezebel's witchcraft will operate as "spiritual groupies," travelling to various meetings, churches and conferences in hope of luring some influential leader into her bed of seduction.

The evil spirit of Jezebel hates Kingdom rule and apostolic government. The rebellious Jezebel and her eunuch's defy law and order. Jezebel is motivated to get into positions that are close to the set-leader. Jezebel will attempt to divide the intercessors or prayer team from the visionary leader. Watch for Jezebel to wiggle into positions that have vocal capabilities. Intercessors, worship leaders and prophetic presbyteries are highly sought after areas for Jezebel.

Jezebel will attempt to isolate and disconnect the set-leader from the rest of the flock. This ranges from the Elders of the church to the Pastors own spouse. She will begin to plant seeds of discord through her communication with various leaders, especially the Pastor. She will slander and talk about the Pastor's wife to others. She will lie, saying things like "She doesn't love me," or "I've tried to reach out to her but she's to busy for me."

Jezebel will look to undermine the Pastor's wife. This trickery is carried out in a cunning manner. Jezebel doesn't attack the pastor's wife directly, but rather makes subtle negative comments to others about her that questions her capability to engage in leadership.

Jezebel is a master of the "blame game," and is brilliant in obtaining sympathy and support from those around her by fabricating stories and manipulating the events.

If the pastor does not succumb to her deceptions, the Jezebel will begin to assassinate the Pastor's good character through planting lies about him behind his back.

When Jezebel is attacking a Pastor and a church, watch for signs of discouragement, fatigue, increased and unexplained physical sickness within the congregation and financial distress.

Whether Jezebel tries to control the Pastor in an obvious aggressive manner or in an undercover passive way makes no difference to her, as long as she can gain control.

Apostles must be aware of the spirit of Jezebel operating in women that desires them to fill the void left by their absent or abusive biological father. Apostles are called to be genuine apostolic fathers and spiritual mentors. Jezebel will look to pervert this dimension by playing off of the rejection within the host. Apostolic fathers must guard against this by feeding their spiritual sons and daughters the bread of deliverance.

Jezebel targets and operates through worship leaders.

Jezebel will not only target a Pastor, but she will look to get the Worship leader trapped in her web. The spirit of Jezebel will manifest in an extremely authoritarian and uncompromisingly controlling worship leader. A worship leader with a Jezebel spirit will usually be lured into sustaining several flirtatious relationships with women in the church. Jezebels goal is for these inappropriate relationships to turn into adulterous affairs, eventually destroying the leader, his family, ministry and church.

Pride and arrogance is at the core of leaders that have been sucked into Jezebel's network. Many of these religious tycoons engage in homosexual acts of perversion with men and boys that have been previously abused.

Jezebelic worship leaders and musicians like to control the

service and will sabotage the ministry through various means. Songs played to intentionally depress the atmosphere, faulty equipment and late or missing staff members are some of the methods used.

Praise & worship leaders, choir directors and ministers of music that host the Jezebel spirit are merchandisers that will high-jack churches by placing heavy financial burdens on them. Many are arrogant and prideful leaders that desire to be worshipped themselves. They look to "box-in" a ministry so that the ministry is dependent on them. Many Jezebelic worship leaders will recruit homosexual performers to engage in sex acts with them, and in return provide notoriety and career advancement in the gospel music culture.

Offended People

Offended people are prime targets and candidates to become entrapped into Jezebel's web of witchcraft.

Jezebels motive is disunity, discord and division. Jezebel's desire is to split families and churches. This ancient evil spirit has caused many to stumble through offenses against each other- especially offenses against leaders.

Jezebel deceives those that have been offended into thinking they have a right to hold on to their offense. The spirit of Jezebel will have the host monitor and take account of all past offenses and use them to her benefit when she sees the need for control and manipulation.

Offended people will go from person to person letting everyone know of their offense. It's never their fault and they become highly critical of the one that offended them. Many times offense occurs because the truth was given to a person in a particular area. Religious people take offense when Kingdom truth is presented to them. They are stiff-necked and will not repent. The unwillingness to repent is a hallmark of Jezebel.

Jesus offended many people both in word and action.

And they were <u>offended</u> in him …… Matthew 13:57 (KJV)

Then came his disciples, and said unto him, Knowest thou that the Pharisees were <u>offended</u>, after they heard this saying – Matthew 15:12 (KJV)

Is not this the carpenter, the son of Mary, the brother of James, and Joses, and of Juda, and Simon? and are not his sisters here with us? And they were <u>offended</u> at him – Mark 6:3 (KJV)

Many therefore of his disciples, when they had heard this, said, This is an hard saying; who can hear it? When Jesus knew in himself that his disciples murmured at it, he said unto them, Doth this <u>offend</u> you? – John 6:60-61 (KJV)

Believers are not to take offense. One can only be offended if they walk in un-forgiveness. You cannot walk in love and forgiveness and take an account of a suffered wrong. People that are offended walk in hatred towards others in the body of Christ and their own biological family.

I've found that many ask for the truth but cannot handle the truth. The truth of God's word challenges fleshly mindsets and demonic systems. However, if one becomes offended by the truth, they will quickly make the messenger out to be the enemy.

The Apostle Paul gave the saints in the Galatian church the truth.

Am I therefore become your enemy, because I tell you the truth – Galatians 4:16 (KJV)

Many people do not want to accept personal responsibility for their actions. To them it is much easier to simply point a finger at someone else or the devil. The danger with this mindset is that one can develop a victim mentality and believe that the reason they act the way they do is because of what others have done to them. Jezebel will exploit this mindset to gain a foothold in one's life.

Prayer Groups and Intercessors

Intercession is vital to the life of any church. Jezebel loves to hang out in prayer ministries and connect with "the intercessors". She looks to take control over others in the group by acting ultra spiritual and using terms like, "I'm hearing from God," and demands that others listen to her self described wise-counsel. She paints her face as a concerned believer that can "protect" others from the injustices that exists. Jezebel will eventually suppress the prayers of others and initialize independent teachings that are designed to create soul ties with people suffering from rejection, anger and offense. This eventually creates the web that entangles many into perversion and whoredoms.

Pastors and senior leaders often look to Intercessory prayer team members to uphold and support the vision of the church by praying for the vision and it's leaders. Intercessors who get a different vision than what the Lord spoke to the set leader are prime suspects for operating as a Jezebel. Witchcraft prayers being released by members of the team must be dealt with immediately.

Jezebel can do much damage when she infiltrates the intercessory prayer team. Prayer team members must be held accountable to the set leader and continuously go through deliverance. Unfortunately, I have seen cases where Jezebel has embedded herself into an intercessory prayer team and ultimately turned the entire congregation against its leaders.

The Kingdom of God opposes the spirit of Jezebel. Because the Kingdom of God is governmental it demands Jezebel to be dethroned. In order for people to dethrone Jezebel from their life, they must repent. I have found that intercessors must always be at the forefront of repentance unto the Lord. There are times where intercessors will call for the corporate body to repent. While this is a good thing, it is critical that intercessors go through their own repentance to ensure Jezebel is not up to some religious trick to gain control over leadership and the congregation.

When instructed to repent, those bound by Jezebel will not repent due to their unwillingness to forgive others and submit to authority. Rather they remain soul tied to rejection, rebellion, bitterness and religion.

When prayer is non-existent in a local assembly I can guarantee you that Jezebel has spun her web and created a network of witchcraft. Great discernment must be used to identify the spirit of Jezebel in operation in churches, families, prayer movements, networks and prayer phone lines.

Prophets & Prophetic ministry

Jezebel wants to prevent prophetic ministry, growth and prosperity from going forth. She hates the moves of the Holy Spirit, specifically healing, deliverance and worship. Jezebel hates accurate prophetic ministry and will counterfeit true prophetic operations whenever possible.

Historically, Jezebel desired to kill the prophets of God. In the New Covenant she wants to extinguish, paralyze or control prophetic ministry. Prophetic ministry includes prophecy, dance, creative arts, minstrels and musicians, prayers and intercessions.

Jezebel looks to operate in and control the prophetic ministry of a church. Churches that embrace prophetic ministry will have to contend with the Jezebel spirit because this spirit mimics the prophetic gifts. Jezebel calls herself a prophetess.

Notwithstanding I have a few things against thee, because thou sufferest that woman Jezebel, which calleth herself a prophetess, to teach and to seduce my servants to commit fornication, and to eat things sacrificed unto idols – Revelation

2:20 (KJV)

Jezebel targets people that flow in the prophetic. Jezebel loves personal prophecy and will use it as a vehicle to release her witchcraft and sorcery.

Believers that do not submit to apostolic governmental authority and proper New Testament prophetic operations are high on the list of being used by witchcraft. Proper training in the prophetic and discernment is paramount in identifying potential Jezebel networks from being formed.

Jezebel will prophesy manipulative words over a person's life and combine it with utterances in false tongues. Jezebel has the ability to sound ultra-spiritual and commonly uses a mystical approach when engaged in her witchcrafts.

Jezebel hates genuine and pure prophetic ministry because she hates the voice of God. She will pull out every trick available to block the prophetic dimension from functioning effectively.

Prophetic ministry is capable of doing many things, however three of the most powerful things are:

1) Release saints into their destiny
2) Strengthen the church
3) A call for repentance

Prophets are always targets of Jezebel. She will look to hunt down those that speak the voice of God. Watch for this spirit to target prophets that are not working with Apostles or apostolic teams. Many Prophets that have not been properly trained in the apostolic dimension do not understand the role of a prophet, specifically its correlation with the building ministry of an Apostle in the New Covenant.

Jezebel will use intimidation tactics to suppress the Prophets and prophetic ministry. Because of the powerful anointing that is on the prophetic gift and its ability to strengthen the church, Jezebel will retaliate against those that operate in this gift. Elijah was a mighty Prophet in the Old Testament. He was able to perform many miracles and call fire down from heaven. After Elijah's victorious showdown with the prophets of Baal, Jezebel released a fury of retaliation that had the mighty Prophet run and hide.

And Ahab told Jezebel all that Elijah had done, and withal how he had slain all the prophets with the sword. Then Jezebel sent a messenger unto Elijah, saying, So let the gods do to me, and more also, if I make not thy life as the life of one of them by to morrow about this time. And when he saw that, he arose, and went for his life, and came to Beersheba, which belongeth to Judah, and left his servant there. But he himself went a day's journey into the wilderness, and came and sat down under a juniper tree: and he requested for himself that he might die; and said, It is enough; now, O Lord, take away my life; for I am not better than my fathers – I Kings 19:1-4 (KJV)

Prophets are targets of Jezebel's threats, intimidation and fear tactics. I have found that the spirit of Rejection binds many Prophets.

Hurts, wounds, abuse and past experiences can drive some Prophets to a place of isolation.

It is a dangerous thing for Prophets to operate in self-pity and rejection. Prophets can be deceived into thinking that they are the only one going through persecution and attacks. This mindset contributes to their propensity to withdraw from others and hide in caves.

And he said, I have been very jealous for the Lord God of hosts: for the children of Israel have forsaken thy covenant, thrown down thine altars, and slain thy prophets with the sword; and I, even I only, am left; and they seek my life, to take it away – I Kings 19:10 (KJV)

Jezebel will probe to find any deficiency in your life and get you to want to give up. Prophets must be careful that they do not become depressed, weary and double-minded. Suicide is a spirit that must be guarded against in Prophets.

Undelivered prophets that have not addressed spirits of rejection, shame, abuse, inferiority, guilt, perversions or pride will become like Elijah and take flight from Jezebel's threats. They will become prime targets as they find themselves unable to contend and challenge her witchcrafts. Prophets must go through and maintain high-level deliverance so they can guard against Jezebel's strategic maneuvers.

Chapter Two

Prime Suspects

In this chapter we will look into some of the key identifiers and character traits that goes along with the spirit of Jezebel.

The spirit of Jezebel is much more than what meets the eye, and her operations can become extremely difficult to discern for the untrained eye. With the large amount of believers that transfer from church to church, leaders and believers alike need to be equipped in deliverance ministry.

In my many years of ministry, I have battled the spirit of Jezebel on numerous occasions. I've noticed that she always shows up when there is a shift in the spirit and upgrades are occurring. A season of transition where fresh, new revelation is being released seems to get Jezebel's attention. One of the major things that will agitate her is when the Kingdom of God is preached. Jezebel defies the law of the Lord and government of God. The Kingdom is governmental and rules over all. Kingdom minded ministries are targets for Jezebel. As such, they need to be equipped to recognize her methods of operation.

Jezebel spirits can be in a state of incubation and lay dormant until they are triggered. Once activated, Jezebel will deploy an arsenal of witcheries to masterfully spin her web. Jezebel attacks everyone and will lure those that entertain her tricks of deception into her web. Once entangled, the host is quickly intoxicated with paralyzing venom that binds the soul.

Individuals that have come into agreement with the sprit of Jezebel are severely tormented and must be delivered. However, make no mistake, Jezebel will use any weakness you have to further develop her web of destruction. This includes having compassion towards the host. Certainly, you are dealing with a human being behind the Jezebel spirit, but you cannot be soft and weak towards them. If you suspect that a person is operating with a Jezebel spirit, you must be mature enough to differentiate the person from the demon,

Additionally, one must understand how to delineate between the real Jezebel and whom she's pointing her finger at in an attempt to get the focus off of her. Jezebel is notorious for calling innocent people "Jezebel". This is to deflect any suspicious thoughts against her towards others. Jezebel will also cover up or tamper with any evidence that incriminates her.

A prime suspect is a person that law enforcement personnel believe most probably committed a crime that is under investigation.

There are certain characteristics that always seem to follow those that are bound by the spirit of Jezebel. As previously stated, I have battled this spirit for many years and have been an eyewitness to her methods, operations and manifestations. It is my prayer that by sharing with you some of what I've seen and discerned, that you will be able to identify her in the early stages of her wicked schemes.

Before we explore some of these characteristics to watch out for, I want to point out that simply because someone has one or two of these traits does not necessarily prove that they are operating as a Jezebel host. Ultimately, the spiritual gift of discernment of spirits is needed. However, these leading indicators will assist you in monitoring and guarding your church, business, family and marriage from the plans of Jezebel.

Jezebelic behaviors

Stealth like deception

Jezebel's greatest asset is to remain hidden. One of the things Jezebel wants to do is blend in and remain undetected. She is like a chameleon in the spirit. Her highly developed ability to appear one way with a select group of people, yet operate in a completely different way with another group causes a whirlwind of confusion. Jezebel initially comes across as the innocent bystander to minor problems that have been irritating you. However over time, you will find out that together with her companion Ahab and trusty eunuch's, she is at the heart of the confusion.

Jezebel will cause commotion within the church by planting seeds of suspicion and pairing individuals against each other. Be on guard for those that want to get in your ear and say things such as, "these people do not appreciate you."

Jezebel has perfected the art of lying. This spirit can manipulate the host and its victims and make them believe up is down and right is left.

Jezebel targets new converts, new church members and visitors. By concealing herself as a "watchman," she will deploy spirits of suspicion and label those that genuinely want the Kingdom of God as "troublemakers" or even a Jezebel themselves. Many times this is done disguised as "discernment," nevertheless it is undeniably a tactic released to isolate the ministry from those not tainted by Jezebels toxic venom.

Jezebel will deploy deception demons and spirits of delusion and bind the host so deep, that the host believes that the lie is the truth. This makes the host with the Jezebel spirit feel as they're okay and that everyone else is wrong.

Jezebel will lie against those in authority in an effort to get others to speak evil of leadership. Her desire is that the person they lied to will take the bait and start talking to others about leadership. When the leader of the church or ministry hears about this and questions the parties' involved, Jezebel will be nowhere to be found. Essentially, she drops the bomb, watches it explode and then asks, "what happened?"

As long as Jezebel gets her way, she's fine and will remain under the radar screen. However, if and when she doesn't get her way, watch out, she will manifest through the host in numerous and vicious ways.

Reconnaissance and information gathering

Jezebel uses information to obtain power. She loves controlling her victims by gathering personal and confidential information about them by convincing them that she is the only one that can be trusted. She controls her prey through obtaining knowledge about shameful secrets and embarrassing incidents. Information gathering is used to keep her eunuchs in her bedchamber so they can do her bidding as needed.

Information gained about leaders is used to assassinate their character, discredit their integrity and methodically dismantle ministries and families. Jezebel will gossip and tell everyone's business after you confide in her.

Jezebel desires information and she will have her host sequester information from people. She hungers to be the first to know and wants to know everything that is going on. This is due to the Jezebelic networks assault to gain strategic control of the lines of communication between individuals and leaders.

Jezebel uses information as a weapon and will pair people (even family members) against each other. Jezebel wants to impress key leaders and get into the circle of influence to ultimately remove the authority. Jezebel is a bragger and namedropper. In the apostolic & prophetic culture she will use all of the buzzwords and spiritual terminology but clearly opposes the Kingdom of God.

She loves to be in possession of information and she will pressure you for information through constant phone calls and lengthy conversations that will eventually wear you out.

It doesn't take a lot of information; just a small amount will go a long way as Jezebel inserts her own opinions into the facts. She seems to know everything about everyone. Watch out for people that others point to when you want to know something. Those that can readily provide intimate details about people's past, their actions or whereabouts, could be a prime suspect in hosting the Jezebel spirit.

Never give Jezebel any personal information, especially about your family and past. Do not tell her about what personal challenges you are going through, how you are feeling, or what God is doing in you life. Do not share any personal revelation, vision or dreams with her. Married couples must be particularly careful not to share private information regarding their relationship with each other or information regarding their children.

Be very cautious when someone says, "I've always wanted to meet you." Jezebel will use flattery and will uncover any amount of pride in you your life and will use it against you.

Monitor people that you've only known for a short period of time that begin to want to get closer to you. Statements such as, "I want you to reveal your heart to me" or "I want to get to know you better", is very dangerous and an indicator that a Jezebelic operation may be in development. It may sound good, but it's not God. Jezebel is probing to locate something that she can use against you. Knowing one's heart is not important. Discernment of spirits is.

For from within, out of the heart of men, proceed evil thoughts, adulteries, fornications, murders, - Mark 7:21 (KJV).

If Jezebel cannot get information from you directly, she will send in a reconnaissance team to gather intelligence.

Jezebel has her own children that will run around and manufacture conversations with key people or eavesdrop on group meetings. I've seen cases where the host has stood outside my office when I was having a meeting with a person simply to obtain information.

Jezebel will become friends with those you communicate with the most, specifically those on your leadership team. Board members, apostolic and prophetic team members and administrators are all likely targets for information gathering.

Jezebel will show up at meetings uninvited and say something like: "I thought you wanted me here". She will follow the Pastor, his wife and those close to him wherever they go. If Jezebel does not have the information needed she will use guilt as a form of manipulation by saying things like, "I feel as though I'm not involved enough" or "no one communicates to me and I feel so unwanted." These are classic Jezebelic tactics used to break down any resistance to her bewitchments.

Jezebel will extract information out of you and use it against you. She will twist and turn your words and wrangle information to enhance her agenda. Tactically she implements lying, crying, whining, accusing, tale bearing, self-pity and anything else to weaken you. Her desire is for you to operate in the flesh through the emotions. If you are around a person or group that always "takes you there", you may be under attack from the spirit of Jezebel.

If you find yourself donating information to a person yet you know deep inside that you should not be providing that level of information, you might be communicating with a Jezebel host.

Interestingly enough, a Jezebelic host will share pieces of information with you too. Much of what was told to you was most likely told to the host in confidence by someone else. This gives the Jezebelic host a sense of power and importance even to the extent of trying to impress people by appearing as if she "knows everything," specifically what others do not know.

Jezebel will share some very personal and intimate things with you about her life. In an effort to gain your confidence, she will appear sincere, honest and transparent. She will begin to cry and weep about how she has no one to talk to and that no one understands her, but you. She wants you to sympathize with her so can lure you into her web of seduction and become allies.

Jezebel's network will extrapolate any information you provide and search for areas of emotional scars. Once identified, Jezebel will attempt to open the wound and develop a soul-tie with you.

To break away from this manipulation, you must find genuine leadership that you can open up to and share your heart with. Quality leaders and apostolic fathers will minister the truth of God's word to you in the spirit of love, mercy and kindness, rather than control you or manipulate you with information they received.

Drama Queens

Jezebel is a drama queen. She demands a lot of attention and can wear you out. Hosts that operate with a Jezebel spirit are capable of putting on dramatic theatrical performances that are second to none. When she is performing at her best you may find yourself caught in a whirlwind of confusion, turmoil and strife.

Jezebel exaggerates everything. She is capable of creating a crisis out of thin air. Her lies and treachery will move from person to person as she makes statements such as, "Everyone is saying this" or "Everyone sees we have a problem."

Jezebel's drama is never ending. She will turn every concern that anyone has about her into an accusation that she is being attacked. When Jezebel is challenged or cornered she will always turn the table and say that she was under attack due to the heavy anointing on her life.

Jezebel is a liar. She has mastered the art of lying insomuch that if you're not operating at a high level of discernment, you will believe her lies and potentially hurt good people. Jezebel's acting will have you thinking that she is on your side and everyone else is against you.

Through her artistries she will begin to launch accusations against others. She will begin to blame you and others for problems that exist. Since she can do no wrong, she will accuse one of being prideful or tolerant of specific individuals.

Jezebel is a master at playing the "blame game" and will

bring forth extremely convincing arguments and accusations to build her case. Jezebel will twist, wrangle and pervert information to suit her, even if it involves lying and crying. She will do anything to make you appear to be the guilty party. Her goal is for you to begin to lash out and cut people off. Anyone that threatens her plans becomes a target of her attack.

Jezebel is the exemplification of witchcraft, idolatry, manipulation, discouragement and perversion, and will take matters into her own hands to undermined authority.

Talkative and vocal

Jezebel uses excessive talking as a form of control, manipulation and a technique to bring confusion into a situation.

In general, Jezebel does all the talking. It does not matter what the topic is, you can be sure that Jezebel will look to dominate the discussion. This is due to her hunger for control and to be in the spotlight. She will not receive input from anyone in her life. All conversations with her are strictly one-sided.

Beware of individuals that deplete your time by using you as a sounding board and "talking your head off". Those bound by Jezebel will talk so much that after their finished; you will be completely confused or totally depressed. Watch for signs of extreme fatigue and feelings of being drained. Migraine headaches or intense eye pressure have been reported after encounters with Jezebel. If you feel like you want to "hrow in the towel after someone talks to you, it's a sure sign of a Jezebelic attack.

Additionally, Jezebel loves the microphone. She desires to have an audience and understands the power of her threatening's. She desires a platform to release accusations against the brethren. Once she get's rolling, there is no stopping her.

Who hath sent out the wild ass free? or who hath loosed the bands of the wild ass – Job 39:5 (KJV)

Jezebel is strategically aligned with the wild ass spirit and desires a pasture to feed from and ultimately the platform from which she will work. Jezebel hungers for the microphone and releases word curses camouflaged under the prophetic anointing. Remember, Jezebel calls herself a prophetess. I have seen many times where prophetic witchcraft is release by Jezebel or one of her prophets. Yes, Jezebel has prophets.

Now therefore send, and gather to me all Israel unto mount Carmel, and the prophets of Baal four hundred and fifty, and the prophets of the groves four hundred, which eat at Jezebel's table – I Kings 18:19 (KJV)

Those that eat at Jezebel's table are the prophets of witchcraft. Baal is the god of prophetic divination. This spirit ushers people into idolatry under the disguise of religion.

Jezebel will look to kill genuine prophetic ministry and raise up prophetic sects through deception.

But evil men and seducers shall wax worse and worse, deceiving, and being deceived – II Timothy 3:13 (KJV)

Once deceived through Jezebel's trickeries, the host will commence to release witchcraft through controlling prayers and false prophetic unction's and spells.

Witchcraft is primarily released through words and Jezebel loves to talk. She will sound ultra-spiritual in her prophetic sorcery. The Jezebel spirit will play with the name of God and use it as a novelty by excessively using terms such as, "God told me," or "I saw this" and "I heard the spirit say." Remember, just because someone says its God doesn't mean it is God.

Control & Manipulation

Control and manipulation are the fiercest parts of the Jezebel spirit. Jezebel is a megalomaniac that has an appetite for power. She is the ultimate controller and a masterful manipulator.

Control and manipulation is witchcraft. A craft is a skill, and Jezebel is highly skilled at controlling and manipulating people. To control someone is to direct their behavior or focus in order to get them to do what you want. When you're in control, you have power over something. For example, if you're directing the automobile to turn a certain way and accelerate to a certain speed, then you are in control of it.

Manipulation is to control someone by crafty or deceptive means, especially to one's own advantage and for a particular purpose.

Jezebel will attempt to manipulate you through random statements to others that portray you as non-compassionate or unwilling to embrace them. Her strategy is having this information get back to you and break you down through empathy towards her. Always a masterful performer, she will play the rejected role to gain sympathizers and seduce vulnerable people into her bedchamber.

Jezebel uses other people as hostages where and when it suits her needs. The objective is to secure power, influence and control. Once she establishes a fortified stronghold where she is in command, she will typically assassinate her hostages through betrayal, rejection and sabotage.

Jezebel is a murderer of the family and she works extremely hard to gain control of all family decisions. If in a female, Jezebel will identify and gravitate to other women in the family that have experienced marital problems or have been hurt and abused by men. A woman married to a man that harbors the Ahab spirit is a prime target.

This spirit is a man-hater that lusts for power. Jezebel uses seductive female attributes and exploits men in every possible way. Her silky smooth speech, soft touch and charming behavior is a type of narcotic designed to weaken her prey before devouring them in her web of perversion.

Controlling wives

Jezebelic wives have no problem with publicly humiliating their husbands with a harsh tongue or rolling eyes. Watch for wives that talk to their husbands in a condescending manner to simply demonstrate to everyone who's really in charge.

A Jezebel wife will deny her husband the right to an intimate relationship with his spouse simply to maintain control over her husband through the marriage bed. Over time she will reward his obedience and submission to her dominance with sexual gratification. Generally she is not really interested in sex but uses it as a manipulative tool. To Jezebel, sex is a tool that can be used to gain power and control.

Whether it's a wife refusing to have sex with her husband for manipulative purposes, or using sex as a means to draw one more powerful than her into a compromised position that will cause their destruction or downfall, Jezebel's seduction is all about gaining supremacy.

Jezebel will use children in a relationship as instruments of manipulation to control her husband and extended family members.

Jezebel may use another trick of deception and openly accuse her husband of not assuming the leadership role of the family. She will act as if she is trying to submit to him, however because he is not acting like a man, she has to take the lead. This is nothing more than another hoax to remain in stealth mode while she undermines her husband's authority.

Some indicators of controlling wives are:

- Talking for her husband and telling people how he feels and what he thinks.
- Talking in a condescending and disrespectful matter or talking over her husband.

- Treating her husband like a child by doing everything for him.
- Saying she's the spiritual head of the home because her husband is ill equipped.
- Talking in public about what he doesn't do in order to motivate him to do something.
- Makes all the decisions in the home because she feels her husband can't do anything right.
- Sulks until she gets her way
- Independence – she states she doesn't need her husband and makes certain he knows it.
- Criticizes everything her husband does
- Shuts down or gives her husband the cold shoulder when things don't go her way.
- Gives her husband the evil eye when he talks to others independent of her.
- Yells, screams or emotionally freaks out over small things.
- Deprives her husband of sex, conversation and companionship if he doesn't do what she wants.

Controlling Husbands

If a male, Jezebel will usually look for arrogant, pompous and prideful men. Men that have served in the military are very susceptible to Jezebels snare.

Jezebel will deceive men into using scriptures to manipulate their wife into submission. I've seen men take the text found in Ephesians chapter 5 and Hebrews chapter 13 out of context and demand their wife submits to their every desire. Many times this consists of perversion in the bedroom and domestic duties that render the wife exhausted, while the husband watches television in his man-cave.

Watch for men that control all the money but do not provide for their own wife. I've seen men that take their wife's entire paycheck, pay the bills but never give their wife any money. Many of them have all the latest and greatest electronic equipment or dress up like a GQ model, but their wife looks like she's been thrown away.

Jezebelic husbands will use money, fear and intimidation as a tool of manipulation and control, ultimately getting the wife to perform at his satisfactory level.

Jezebelic husbands will always look to keep their wife busy, running errands and keeping them away from any type of social life. This is a form of control and is designed to keep the wife from achieving anything in life.

Some indicators of controlling husbands are:

- Monitors his wife's behaviors, making sure she is always where she said she would be and doing what she said she would be doing
- He makes his wife give him an account for every single action she takes and dollar she spends
- Controls all credit cards, car keys, and bank accounts
- Keeps his wife from family, friends or experiencing events outside of the home.
- Uses violent threats to control and intimidate his wife
- Punches holes in walls.
- Calls his wife dumb, stupid, lazy, fat, skinny or ugly.
- Checks his wife phone calls and reads her text messages and email.
- Wants his wife to engage in sex "on-demand" for his pleasure and at his convenience.

- Makes statements like "a woman's place is in the kitchen."
- Forbids the wife from pursuing her dreams to take care of him.

Controlling tactics

Jezebel's method of choice is to control her victim by seduction. She will use flattery, smooth prophetic sayings, pleasant words and seducing tears to lure one into her web. If that tactic is unsuccessful she will utilize fear to keep her victim in a place of submission and obedience.

Jezebel knows how to capitalize on the secret emotional hurts and wounds of her host in order to manipulate and control them. Once controlled, she looks to create deep ties with other people that have experienced similar circumstances. As she hypnotizes her prey through false compassion she will immediately labor to isolate them.

Jezebel loves to pull people to herself and away from those who can truly speak into their lives. She is compelled to draw people to herself and will never point people to Jesus. Jezebel will use the power of isolation to separate her victims from positive relationships, genuine apostolic fathers and powerful equipping centers.

Jezebel will use prayer to manipulate the one she is attempting to control, especially loud public prayers. Jezebel will release prayers over that person to create the illusion that she (Jezebel) is obedient to God and that other people do not care.

Jezebel loves to pray and be seen of men.

And when thou prayest, thou shalt not be as the hypocrites are: for <u>they love to pray</u> standing in the synagogues and in the corners of the streets, that they may be <u>seen of men</u> .... Matthew 6:5 (KJV)

Jezebelic control also materializes, as the hurting and rejected person is looking for love so bad that when they believe they've found it they become fearful of losing it.

Jezebel has absolutely no sympathy towards her victims. However, she will give the impression that she is sympathetic simply as a means to seduce and control them. Once they're controlled, Jezebel will use self-rejection as a tool to manipulate others into having sympathy towards her.

One of the cunning and crafty operations of witchcraft is in the area of connecting people to each other. Controlling Jezebel spirits will always look to pair people up with each other, thus keeping them controlled. One must be very careful, as this is part of the network and the black widows web of entanglement.

Jezebel will position two people against each other to get her way. For example, I had a situation where my wife and I were invited to be the speakers at a church. It was an out of town ministry and we decided to drive. A prophet at our ministry said she felt the Lord was telling her to travel with us so that she could intercede while we ministered. Honestly it sounded very spiritual. Her next move was to inquire with me about riding in our car to get to the meeting because her car was not in shape to drive that far.

Now, when I travel in my car for a long distance, I like to be free from all stress. As such, I typically will not take on any passengers. I enjoy uninterrupted time travelling together with my wife. However, this person said God was instructing her to "cover us." Rather than saying no, I proceeded to tell the person to ask my wife if it was okay with her. Well, she ended up travelling with us. The ride there and back was filled with her complaining to my wife and I about everyone at and in the ministry. By the time we got home my wife and I were exhausted and had a feeling of having been drained of joy and peace.

Over the next couple of days we began to accuse each other of having permitted this person to travel with us. My wife then asked me, "Why did you give her permission to travel with us?" Of course my response was, "I didn't give her permission, I simply told her to go ask you." My wife then stated, "that's not what she told me." She (the person that traveled with us) said, "Apostle said it's okay that I travel with you guys, if it's okay with you." This was a classic case of Jezebel pitting my wife and I against each other in order to get her way.

Another approach Jezebel uses is to imply that everyone disapproves of her. This is a tactic to get those she is looking to bring under her control to feel as if they cannot express an opinion for fear of disapproving her.

A Jezebelic host will accuse everyone that objects to her ways as being evil towards her. Jezebel will make herself to be the target of your inability to truly understand her. She will often accuse you of judging her based on other people's opinions.

Finally, if you ever break your commitment to someone who is caught up in Jezebel's web, there will immediately be retaliation against you in the form of manipulation. This is designed to get you to operate against your will and line up with Jezebel's controlling agenda. Jezebel is never concerned about your will but only her evil plots of witchcraft.

Volunteers

Another method to securing and maintaining control is for Jezebel to volunteer and take assignments that are critical to a church or ministry. Behind the scenes Jezebel is feverishly laboring to gain control of strategic areas in an attempt to impede the church from walking in the spirit. This includes gaining control of sensitive information, such as passwords and legal documents.

She will energetically volunteer to lead the congregation in a call to prayer and fasting or some other activity simply to look important and spiritual.

Jezebel will volunteer to make important flight, hotel or other travel arrangements for incoming guest speakers with the intention of making a connection with that leader. Once the task is complete, she will boast to others how she knows that person.

Jezebel will look to befriend the "target" on Facebook and initiate the process of manipulation through sending instant messages to that person. These messages are designed to break the relationship the leaders have with each other and usher in discord and division.

I've seen many situations where the Jezebelic host will volunteer for things that they have absolutely no intention to follow through on. When asked how things are going, they will act as if progress is being made. Down the road, as the completion of the task becomes more critical they will exhibit signs of dementia, and say something like, "I don't recall you saying that." Jezebel will lie and say, "don't you remember you told me to not do that." This is designed to bring confusion and to sabotage the project or event.

Another tactic is to play the blame game and demonize others. Jezebel will blame those around her, claiming she did not get the support needed to complete the task.

Remember, Jezebel will never admit to being wrong and will always look to justify her behaviors. To accept responsibility would go against the prideful witch that she is. When a Jezebel apologizes it is never in true repentance or genuine admitting of a wrongdoing, but rather will place blame on you by saying, "I'm sorry your feelings were hurt" or "I'm sorry you feel that way."

Finally, Jezebel is lazy and slothful.

Not slothful in business; fervent in spirit; serving the Lord – Romans 12:11 (KJV)

A Jezebelic host quickly loses enthusiasm and excitement for assigned of volunteered tasks. They are notorious for sinking into a state of being slow, boring, sluggish, dull, and uninterested in the vision of the church. They act as if they are so busy, but yet do absolutely nothing.

Gift Giving

Gift giving is another form of control and manipulation that a Jezebel host will use to get you to feel obligated to communicate with her. Gifts are given with the intent of having the targeted victim compromise the truth and not confront this evil spirit.

Be aware that Jezebelic hosts will do pleasant things for you. For example, she will buy you gifts, pay for a vacation, and drop off groceries to your house for the sole purpose of getting you to feel comfortable around her. Her desire is to get you to feel relaxed in her presence and begin to open up with her.

Jezebel wants you to feel as if you owe her something. She will go out of her way to ensure that you know she is giving her time and money into the ministry. She has no problem being the largest donor in the church.

When Jezebel gives there are many strings attached. Watch for people that are always talking about how much they give or sacrifice for the vision. Additionally, individuals that make a spectacle when they give by placing the gift (offering) in your hand or calling you later in the day and saying "I forgot to give my offering, can I send it to you," could be using giving as a tool to manipulate and control you.

Manipulation in the area of giving extends throughout Jezebel's network and offspring. When Jezebel does not get her way, she will instruct her network of thugs to withhold giving. This demonic racketeering is an intimidation tactic designed to bring fear to the leader so Jezebel can obtain what she wants – power!

Certainly not everyone that gives gifts or forgets to put heir offering in the collection receptacle is guilty of being a Jezebel. Most people's motives are pure when they give. They give cheerfully and faithfully support the vision of the House of God. However, discernment must be in operation to guard against the tactic of using gift giving as a means to control.

It might take weeks, months or in some cases even years, but eventually you will be reminded of what Jezebel has done for you or given to you. Don't be surprised if a Jezebelic host contacts you weeks after being exposed or separated from your ministry to remind you of how much time, money and resources they gave.

This form of manipulation does not only occur in churches, it is in families, marriages and businesses also.

In families, a controlling mother may constantly remind her son/daughter of the sacrifice she made in raising them. A statement such as, "I went without so you could have a better life," is an example. Children can be used also. Other siblings that remind their younger brother/sister of the things they did for them can be used as a form of control. A statement such as, "How can you tell me no when I was the one that changed your diapers while mom and dad were at work," is an example.

In a marriage a Jezebelic husband may use his position of providing for his wife as a method of control. Husbands that purchase gifts for their spouse yet always reminds her of the purchase or sacrifice he made, is displaying Jezebelic patterns. A threat of taking the gift back if the spouse does not comply with Jezebel's demands is witchcraft.

Clearly, giving is something we should all practice. However, there should never be any strings attached or expectation of some favorable return. If there is, Jezebel is at work.

Jedi mind tricks

Jezebel targets those that are weak-minded because they are easily influenced. She seeks out other individuals that she feels she can control and dominate. Jezebel will utilize "Jedi mind tricks" to cause you to perform in a totally uncharacteristic manner.

Jezebel plays these mind tricks to get you to think your doing something wrong. You may feel as if you are losing your sanity. She will do things like showing up at your house or office and say, "I'm here for our meeting," although a meeting was never scheduled. She will insist that you confirmed the meeting or she will blame it on a staff member. "I texted you" or "You must have forgotten," are some common statements. This trickery is to catch you off guard and get you to question yourself. Jezebel uses the element of surprise to stay one step ahead of you.

Think it not strange when you begin to engage in activities that are not a part of your vision. For instance, you may hear the statement, "We're not a loving church and need more fellowship with each other." While fellowship is a very important part of the local church, your vision may not have fellowship as a high priority. Jezebel will trick you into thinking that another activity is needed simply to frustrate you. You'll find yourself doing things you were never called to do.

I've had situations where the Jezebel host would say to me that the church is not praying or fasting enough. While she has no real interest in fasting and praying, it is a tactic to drop everything and move in another direction. Jezebel is a hindering spirit designed to stop you from progressing in what God assigned you to do.

Jezebel's mind tricks are designed to implement her own agenda. Beware of people that have their own ministry agenda. One of the ways Jezebel's agenda is implemented is through calling a corporate fast or corporate prayer. Jezebelic fasting and prayers have nothing to do with the Spirit of God and are designed to deceive many and ultimately bring harm to individuals, ministries and churches. These demonic fasts and calls to prayer are platforms for evil declarations, decrees and prophetic witchcrafts. Unless the senior leader of the ministry has issued a call for corporate prayer and fasting, don't engage in it. It's demonic and perverse.

Jezebel called a fast in the name of her husband Ahab to get Naboth killed because they both wanted something from Naboth that didn't belong to them.

So she wrote letters in Ahab's name, and sealed them with his seal, and sent the letters unto the elders and to the nobles that were in his city, dwelling with Naboth. And she wrote in the letters, saying, Proclaim a fast, and set Naboth on high among the people: And set two men, sons of Belial, before him, to bear witness against him, saying, Thou didst blaspheme God and the king. And then carry him out, and stone him, that he may die. And the men of his city, even the elders and the nobles who were the inhabitants in his city, did as Jezebel had sent unto them, and as it was written in the letters which she had sent unto them – I Kings 21:8-11 (KJV)

Many times a Jezebelic hosts will call a fast for things that do not belong to them. Fasting for a husband or wife although that person is already married is a type of Jezebelic fast.

Much of Jezebel's mind tricks are camouflaged with mysticism and hyper-spiritual rhetoric. She employs "familiar spirits" to seek out those that want more of God. Believers that do not know who they are in Christ or the authority they have in the new covenant are prime targets for her mesmerizing tricks. For instance, she will tell you what you've been thinking. Jezebel operates in clairvoyance and a false Holy Spirit. She will tell you that she sees you in dreams and visions. All of this is to get you to think that she has a special place in your life as a type of guardian.

Jezebel will use Jedi mind tricks to gather followers to get them to eat from her table. She will look for those that are weak, wounded, or those who are in rebellion (witchcraft) and resisting established spiritual authority. Any opposition to Jezebel's mind tricks will result in her manifesting and releasing threatening accusations against the saints. She will quickly make you out to be the bad guy, even accusing you of harboring the spirit of Jezebel yourself.

Finally, watch for Jezebel to pull you into an argument. Remember she is the author of confusion and strife. One of her tricks is to get you to referee a dispute or quarrel that she is having with someone else. She will use spiritual terms such as "I know you're a man (or woman) of God and operate in great discernment." This is a tactic used by her to simply drag you in. Her goal is to get you frustrated by all the confusion and silliness.

Jezebel in your House

People that visit you at your house but never know when to leave will wear you out. This could be an indication of witchcraft and a Jezebel Spirit in operation.

"Withdraw thy foot from thy neighbor's house lest he be weary of thee and so hate thee" - *Proverbs 25:17 (KJV)*

Friends and family members that host the spirit of Jezebel will look to physically enter your home and never leave. They are like roaches. Once in, they take over and are extremely hard to get rid of.

Jezebelic hosts will seek to infiltrate the home environment to bring in confusion and turmoil. Once in, they will set up shop and start attacking and undermining literally every single thing they can. Your home is supposed to be a place of peace and safety. However, once Jezebel is invited in, she will cause major dissension and strife even among the best of friends and family. This spirit is a major peace disturber and it will cause all kinds of havoc and trouble in the family unless it is quickly dealt with and exposed.

This Jezebel spirit will have hosts make demands on the homeowner to financially drain them. Special types of foods, cosmetic or structural changes to the house, cable boxes, garage space and furniture are some of the demands she will place on you to accommodate her needs. She will have you running her errands and babysitting her children often. She will borrow your car, keep it all day and then return it empty. She will stay up late at night watching television or talking on the phone, keeping you from getting any sleep or rest. All of this is designed to drain you emotionally.

Bottom line - never let a person with a Jezebel spirit in operation move into your house or apartment!

Chapter Three

Harboring the fugitive

Jezebel's network of demons is highly proficient in it's devises as it is strategically aligned with the underworld of darkness. Make no mistake about it, Jezebel's network spreads wide and penetrates deep. Her goal is to bring severe damage to individuals, families, churches, businesses and governments.

Jezebel is sly, cunning and crafty. Therefore, most people do not know that the spirit of Jezebel is exploiting them. Many good people that sincerely love the Lord support the spirit of Jezebel to work her sorceries through them.

The average believer has not been sufficiently equipped to identify and guard against the spirit of Jezebel. Lack of knowledge in this area is destroying many lives.

My people are destroyed for lack of knowledge ..... Hosea 4:6 (KJV)

Jezebel operates through relationships, conversations, lifestyles, emails, Facebook posts and text messages. Many people are bewitched and believe what they are doing is right. This is called deception.

Those that harbor Jezebel may seem very soft-spoken, giving the illusion of being concerned, motherly, protective, even appearing very submissive. They appear to be "on the team" and concerned about things being in order.

In churches, Jezebel works through our brothers and sisters. This is where dealing with the spirit of Jezebel becomes complex.

Most Christians have a difficult time contending with the Jezebel spirit because they do not detached the host (person) from the spirit. As such, they have a propensity to be weak in confronting the host and in turn, end up providing the spirit of Jezebel with a safe-haven by which it can set up it's network.

You must never sympathize with a Jezebelic host. You must be fully resolved to be in direct opposition to her. Any sympathy will be seen as a weakness and used against you. Those that do not confront, contend and expose the spirit of Jezebel are harboring this evil spirit.

God speaks expressly against this ancient evil spirit and demands set-leaders to eradicate the spirit from the churches. The 1st century church in Thyatira had done many good works for the Lord. Unfortunately they were weak and did not expose or root-out the spirit of Jezebel from the church. Rather they permitted her to operate and seduce the saints.

Notwithstanding I have a few things against thee, because thou sufferest that woman Jezebel, which calleth herself a prophetess, to teach and to seduce my servants to commit fornication, and to eat things sacrificed unto idols – Revelation 2:20 (KJV)

Those that do not challenge or expose this ancient spirit are not on the side of the Lord.

As leaders we must be exceptionally strong and courageous in our dealings with this spirit. Be aware that when someone is harboring a Jezebel spirit, they are *"de facto,"* preparing to take you down. However, please remember that we are wrestling with demons, not people. We are to be tenacious toward demons, but firm and loving toward people.

That said we should understand that the host must still be dealt with. Unfortunately, most believers and churches do not engage in genuine deliverance ministry. Contributing to the spiritual deficiencies in our churches is the lack of apostolic equipping and a revelation of the Kingdom of God.

The number of Christians that I have heard say things such as, "a Christian can't have demons," or "it doesn't take all that," saddens me. This mindset in and of itself is part of Jezebel's witchcraft released against the church to create a tolerance to her whoredoms.

This spirit is clever and sneaky. It knows how to make leaders look like the bad guy while making the person controlled by Jezebel look like the victim. Vanguard leaders and churches that oppose and expose the spirit of Jezebel through preaching and demonstration of the Kingdom may be labeled as, "unloving" or "attacking the flock." In one of my battles with Jezebel the host accused me of not being "merciful."

Do not be merciful towards Jezebel, thinking that she will submit to the Word of God. She will not submit. The name Jezebel means "without cohabitation." Moreover, the host harboring the evil spirit is totally deceived and operating in rebellion to God's authority.

When someone is deceived they believe in something that is not true. Jezebel is a master deceiver. Her story lines and scripts are laced with red herrings that lure many into her web.

But evil men and seducers shall wax worse and worse, deceiving, and being deceived - 2 Timothy 3:13 (KJV)

Rebellion is witchcraft and can never be tolerated.

For rebellion is as the sin of witchcraft, and stubbornness is as iniquity and idolatry .... – I Samuel 15:23 (KJV)

Remember, Jezebel wants to blend in and remain undetected. She rides on the backs of Christians that are sympathetic to the host. If you know someone that is operating as a Jezebel or one of her children, you must temporarily break off fellowship with them. You cannot fellowship with the person being used by the Jezebel spirit or the one being lured into her network. You must treat them as someone who lives in disobedience and mark them as such.

Now I beseech you, brethren, <u>mark them</u> which cause divisions and offences contrary to the doctrine which ye have learned; and <u>avoid them</u>. For they that are such serve not our Lord Jesus Christ, but their own belly; and by good words and fair speeches <u>deceive the hearts of the simple</u> – Romans 16:17-18 (KJV)

You cannot play with a host that is operating with the spirit of Jezebel. Jezebel and her network must be taken extremely seriously. Those, whom Jezebel has managed to seduce or recruit to serve in her bedchamber as eunuchs, require extensive deliverance. Deliverance comes from exposure and a demand for genuine repentance.

When it comes to Jezebel, you can forget about simply praying for the host to come to truth and repentance. You're wasting your time. Jezebelic hosts are mesmerized by her seduction and diabolically deceived. Don't be deceived into thinking that you can pray the stronghold out.

Additionally, it is impossible to have a logical conversation with a person bound by a Jezebel spirit. Jezebel uses confusion as a strategy and will twist every conversation, email and text message. Never attempt to counsel with Jezebel. She will run circles around you and you'll end up frustrated, drained and operating out of the flesh. Carnal weapons will not yield any success. This is a spiritual battle.

Eunuchs

The Jezebel spirit has closely aligned offspring called eunuchs. These eunuchs have no strength of their own but rather carry out the witchcraft of Jezebel. They are typically weak-minded individuals that look to the controlling witch for approval, identity, instruction, confirmation and companionship. Jezebel will assimilate people who typically are emotionally dependent on others to make up for their own wounded spirit.

Eunuchs entangled in Jezebel's web of deception will be found operating in false discernment whereby they speak words acquired from Jezebel and not from the Spirit of God. They will be sent on assignment to key people as spiritual spies or terrorists. Many of Jezebel's eunuchs release spells and curses against families, ministries and leaders.

Eunuchs are slaves to Jezebel. Most eunuchs gravitated towards Jezebels bed of perversion because of their elevated levels of rejection and rebellion. Jezebel lures them in through various manipulative tactics and false compassion. Her ultimate goal is control. Once entangled, the Jezebelic host may begin to use controlling statements such as, "you can only be my friend if you do _____."

Jezebel likes to isolate her offspring and keep them away from those not in the network. If you find yourself connected to a person that is unwilling to share you with anyone else, chances are that person is a Jezebel attempting to turn you into a eunuch.

Beware of controlling statements that belittle and intimidate you. Eunuchs have an intense desire to be loved and accepted by others. Jezebel will use false compassion and false mothering as a means control her children. She will deposit seeds of doubt by launching manipulative questions like, "why are you going to that church" or, "why are you connected to him?"

Jezebel keeps her Eunuch's close to her and will sacrifice them in turn to remain undetected. She will demand that her eunuch manifest and reveal itself as the cause of problems that have materialized. Because eunuchs can repent, one may think that the problem has been resolved and things are back to normal. Nothing could be further from the truth. Jezebel has you right where she wants you.

Jezebel likes to birth new spiritual children, fresh eunuchs and perverted prophets to eat from her table. She will look for those that are in rebellion, who are fragile, wounded, or those who are contending, bucking, and fighting any established spiritual authority.

Eunuchs are not controlling or involved in developing diabolical plans. They simply are servants that assist Jezebel in executing her plans. They act as guardians and watchers for their mother Jezebel. Jezebel's children will always come to her defense. They feel responsible to explain and justify her actions. They function as defense attorneys in the spirit and feel obligated to let everyone know that she is "really is a good person," and "has a good heart."

When Jezebel is caught and the spirit of Jezebel is being cast out, Jezebel's eunuchs will grieve and lament. I've seen situations where deliverance was happening and Jezebel's eunuchs yelled out, "this isn't how things should be done," or "where is the love?" In another case a eunuch was sitting in the congregation chanting "come back, come back," as deliverance went forth.

And I will kill her children with death ……….. Revelation 2:23 (KJV)

"To kill her children," means anything that Jezebel gives

birth to in her web will be destroyed. When Jezebel is exposed and rooted out, her eunuchs will disconnect from her network or suffer great hardship.

Jezebel will not repent

And I gave her space to repent of her fornication; and she repented not – Revelation 2:21 (KJV)

One of the primary patterns you must be on the watch for is when a person or group is told to repent and they will not. Leaders and congregations must examine their own ways and live a humble life of repentance. You cannot cast out lust when you harbor lust in your own heart.

The Jezebel spirit cannot be tolerated in ministries or families. Either the affected hosts will repent of their wickedness or they will orchestrate an all out encounter to sabotage ministry and destroy your life.

Be on guard for people that cannot receive correction. Jezebel hates to be told she is wrong and will bring to the surface the strongman of rejection that is active in the host's life. Any correction or rebuke is considered an attack against them and perceived as more rejection. I have found that many itinerant prophets and vagabond musicians that are not connected to an apostolic father or apostolic ministry will not receive true correction. They may begin to say things like, "you're not receiving my anointing," or "I hear from God alone."

Typically they will isolate themselves and release a barrage of accusations against authority. Swift, deliberate and decisive action must occur. The conclusion and aftermath of those that will not repent is clearly not a favorable one.

Behold, I will throw her onto a sickbed, and those who commit adultery with her I will throw into great tribulation, unless they repent of her works, and I will strike her children dead - Revelation 2:22 (NJV)

Any genuine kingdom and authentic apostolic ministry will contend with the evil spirit of Jezebel. One of the reasons some pastors, bishops and leaders will not address this spirit is because it typically results in a loss of people. Individuals that operate with a Jezebel Spirit or are connected to the network itself can become offended in teaching that contends with the spirit. I have been in situations where I have had to expose somebody publicly and told them they are operating as a Jezebel. You cannot be fearful to do this. The host will either receive their deliverance by repenting or become offended and fleeing from the truth.

In all theaters of war, there are casualties. In opposing Jezebel and her network some saints will be wounded. Others may withdraw from the battle and give up. To defeat this spirit you will have to be willing to expose it and address it no matter what, even if it means losing a some close friends, family members or congregations.

Ahab spirits

When looking to dismantle Jezebel's network whether in your church or home, never forget about the Ahab spirit in operation.

Jezebel and Ahab work together as a lethal weapon of mass destruction. These two spirits are very subtle, hidden, poisonous, and unbelievably intelligent. They will do everything to remain concealed. Jezebels greatest power is staying under the radar. Both Jezebel and Ahab are fearful of exposure. Typically, Jezebel will be exposed before Ahab. This is because there can be no Jezebelic without an Ahab. If the Ahab spirit can remain hidden, another Jezebel Queen will be invited in and her network will be rebuilt at a later time, even if it has been temporarily made inoperative.

The Ahab spirit is not stupid. Ahab will team-up with Jezebel's seducing spirit and promote it for his own selfish purposes. However make no mistake. Jezebel is the one steering the ship. She is the ultimate puppet master and has perfected the art of tangling her prey to further her cause.

Ahab is a name that we use in deliverance ministry when we are dealing with the spirit of Jezebel. Of course, in history King Ahab was the ruling King over Israel. King Ahab took Jezebel as his wife from Phoenicia and began to worship the pagan god Baal. Ahab was an evil troublemaker that defiled the entire nation by bringing in perversion, idolatry and whoredoms. Ultimately this led to the nations deterioration and collapse.

And it came to pass, as if it had been a light thing for him to walk in the sins of Jeroboam the son of Nebat, that he took to wife Jezebel the daughter of Ethbaal king of the Zidonians, and went and served Baal, and worshipped him. And he reared up an altar for Baal in the house of Baal, which he had built in Samaria. And Ahab made a grove; and Ahab did more to provoke the Lord God of Israel to anger than all the kings of Israel that were before him – I Kings 16:31-33 (KJV)

Ahab is a companion spirit that is tied to Jezebel. Where you find the spirit of Jezebel, Ahab is there also. Ahab is an enabler to the Jezebel spirit. The Ahab spirit will always manifest first. Without the Ahab spirit, Jezebel would not be able to construct her web of destruction. Ahab permits Jezebel to do her witchcrafts and seduce the church and families.

The Ahab spirit is typically found residing in males and those that have been given authority (although women can host the Ahab spirit also).

Ahab will target those that have a title and position but do not exercise their spiritual or domestic authority. This could be a Pastor, Husband, Boss or anyone else that has a position of delegated responsibility and authority.

As stated, Ahab is an enabler. In the church, a leader that does not institute apostolic order or is fearful of contending and confronting evil is a prime candidate to host the spirit of Ahab. Likewise, a Husband that does not rule his home with a biblical worldview, or acts like a baby, is insecure and arrogant, he could be operating with an Ahab spirit. The Ahab husband will avoid confrontation at all costs and lets his wife have her own way.

Those that operate as an Ahab will tolerate the spirit of Jezebel. Ahab's only concern is that he is able to get his way. For Jezebel to get her foot in the door, she will look for those that she can influence, manipulate and control.

No one else so completely sold himself to what was evil in the LORD's sight as did Ahab, for his wife, Jezebel, influenced him. I Kings 21:25 (NLT)

The primary reason that Jezebel is so proficient in remaining undetected for such a long period of time is due to her affiliation with Ahab. Ahab is an accomplice to Jezebel. The Jezebel spirit in a host will always look to connect with others that have an Ahab spirit. Typically this is someone the fits the mold of a passive, "don't rock the boat" type personality. It's usually a person in some capacity of leadership, perhaps the intercessory prayer team, praise & worship team, Pastor or husband.

Jezebel is fearful of being confronted. This is why she is connected to Ahab. Ahab will never confront Jezebel. If the Jezebelic host is near to being exposed, Jezebel will skillfully twist any situation and run to the Ahab host in an attempt to make the person (the is exposing her) appear to be the one with the controlling Jezebel spirit.

In like manner, when Ahab is confronted, He blames the trouble on other anointed people.

And it came to pass, when Ahab saw Elijah, that Ahab said unto him, Art thou he that troubleth Israel – I Kings 19:17 (KJV)

I have found that this behavior is very common among those that have experienced church hurt or that left their prior church undelivered. When the new ministry confronts this spirit, it will quickly blast leadership as controlling. This is witchcraft and must be rooted out immediately.

Ahab males like toys, attention, success, flattery and sexual perversion. Jezebel is more than willing to accommodate in these areas in order to establish her stronghold.

Watch for men who are prideful and highly driven in their careers. Male leaders that enjoy flattery and praise by females or have strong desires for notoriety are potential hosts for the Ahab spirit.

Sexual perversions are other things that an Ahab host will gravitate to. This is primarily due to the host craving to satisfy the lusts of the flesh. Those bound by an Ahab spirit have minds that are out of control. They have issues such as lust and will engage in various sexual perversions such as pornography, chronic masturbation, homosexuality and adultery. They frequently visit prostitutes and strip bars. Ahab men will justify their actions as if God understands their needs. It is usually a major stronghold in their lives as Jezebel keeps them fed with perverted entertainment and fantasy lusts.

Ahab wants to remain innocent, but is anything but innocent in the eyes of God. He is an evil warlord that enables the spirit of Jezebel to grab hold of the reigns of churches, families and organizations. Ahab harbors the spirit of Jezebel by choosing not to notice, contend and confront when Jezebel is setting up her operation.

Those that harbor the spirit of Jezebel by operating as an Ahab will typically be found having a casual approach towards sin. Leaders that do not oppose sin, evil and perversion are enablers to Jezebel.

Many Ahab's are workaholics, alcoholics and enjoy hanging out with the guys. He will place going to the gym or other social outlets above his parenting and spousal responsibilities. I've found some men will join lodges, fraternities and associations as a means of tuning his wife out. While Ahab has no desire to lead, he does like to criticize those who do.

As previously stated, they are childish and will have temper tantrums when they can't "play." They avoid using their God-given authority to make decisions and are uncertain of their own abilities. Most of the time an Ahab husband will look to his wife (most likely a Jezebel) to make decisions. He may call his wife Mom or Mamma and like more like a son than a husband.

In Ahab's attempt to please his Jezebelic wife he will permit her to have her way. Due to his passivity he will allow her to spend uncontrollably, even to the point of accumulating massive amounts of consumer debt. Rather than confronting his Jezebel wife, the host will shamefully mask his frustration by engaging into some addiction, hobby or perversion. Church leaders that operate in an Ahab spirit will self-medicate the pain by directing all their attention solely on the church or the ministry.

Ahab husbands will turn their heads when they see their wife moving out of her role and responsibility and into his. When a wife plays her husband's role in directing the family, the husband will lose his natural instinct to lead his family.

Jezebel knew that she was not the rightful head, so she invoked her husband's name to give her words authority. Watch for host that harbor Jezebel to "name drop". I've had people use my name when they wanted something done and say to others, "I went to Apostle and he approved it," when I did never give them the okay to do something.

Finally, those that host the Ahab spirit may exhibit characteristics of confusion, disobedience, rebellion, resentfulness, moodiness and greediness. They are known for having outbursts and fits of rage.

Religious spirits

The Jezebel spirit operates as a religious spirit and rules over many religious indoctrination centers, networks and denominations. False teachers, false prophets, and false apostles counterfeit God's order with Jezebelic networks that release an antichrist spirit.

"But why do you let that Jezebel who calls herself a prophet mislead my dear servants into Cross–denying, self–indulging religion" – Revelation 2:20 (Message Bible)

Both Jezebel of the Old Testament and of Revelation functioned under the concealment of religion.

Jezebel makes her bed in religion. Religious churches are safe houses for her fornications. Those that sit in religious controlling churches waiting for things to change subject themselves to Jezebels whoredoms. Embracing religious associations, denominations, networks or iconic leaders is a very dangerous thing. Jezebel is like a black widow spider and will lure you in the bed of religion and use you as an instrument to release her perversions to destroy nations.

Jezebel is a spirit that claims to have religious zeal. She is a master at religious protocol. She will deploy legalistic operations that keep ministries focused on form and fashion, rather than the Holy Spirit. When the Holy Spirit moves among the people of God and their hearts open up to the freedom they have to worship in spirit and in truth. Jezebel will become very agitated and initiate her campaign to suppress liberty.

Her weapon of choice is confusion. She will begin to stir up confusion within the congregation making statements like, "we're becoming to liberal" or "God is not pleased with this." She will target individuals that were involved in movements or denominations that can assist her in her religious escapades. Jezebel uses false holiness as a means of seduction. The bible speaks of putting on a true holiness. The use of the word true implies that there is a false.

And that ye put on the new man, which after God is created in righteousness and true holiness – Ephesians 4:24 (KJV)

False holiness is religious and focuses on the outward appearance and actions rather than the Spirit of God, Grace and the Kingdom. Jezebel will accuse individuals and churches of compromising, when in fact they are simply operating in liberty.

She is a self-proclaimed prophetess that loves being embellished with religious titles. The host may actually have a calling and anointing on his or her life and can appear to have spiritual gifts of prophecy and diverse tongues, but they are corrupted and perverse.

Jezebel is notorious for knowing the latest and greatest in spiritual buzzwords and terminology. Jezebel is into using religious vernacular, hyper-mystical body language and religious clothing. Be on guard for those that give prophetic words but cannot do so without putting on a performance. Religious personnel are polished showmen and Jezebel loves to act out. When she has the opportunity she will shake, slither, blow, jerk, and speak in false tongues.

Loves religion, hates the Kingdom

But woe unto you, scribes and Pharisees, hypocrites! for ye shut up the kingdom of heaven against men: for ye neither go in yourselves, neither suffer ye them that are entering to go in – Matthew 23:13 (KJV)

Religion is a spirit that has corrupted the church for over 2,000 years. It keeps many sincere people out of the Kingdom of God. There are many people that attend religious churches or are aligned with specific denominations that love the Lord. Unfortunately they have been victimized and fallen as prey. They don't know it but they're caught in Jezebel's web.

Jezebel is attracted to religion for many reasons. Clearly, one of them is because the religious spirit will compromise and make concessions simply to avoid persecution and be accepted by other religious peer groups. Religion will never confront Jezebel. Therefore, Jezebel will excel in religious people and churches unrestricted. Jezebel's web of witchcraft operates through religion, denominational sects and racist systems.

Religious denominations are partners with the spirit of racism. Under Jezebel's command, they will ostracize other members in the Body of Christ from attending functions and gatherings. In many cases, these denominations are nothing more than secret societies that were birthed out of rebellion, anger and rejection. They are racially fueled and have divided and segregated the Body of Christ.

Racism is a hateful, murdering spirit that not only works within religious denominations and networks but also in nations and cultures. There are many nations today that have aligned with Jezebel and her witchcrafts. Some of these nations believe that God has chosen them and will use their religion and tradition as the springboard for their hatred against other nations. This has been the catalyst for much slaughtering, butchering, and in some cases the complete genocide of a race.

People that gravitate and associate with the religious culture are perfect candidates to provide a safe-haven for Jezebel to operate in the church and family. Religious culture is not kingdom culture. Religious culture is motivated by the flesh and serves self. The intensity by which it is established is based primarily on tradition. Where religion defines "what you do," tradition defines, "how you do it." Tradition deprives the Word of God from changing people's lives and delivering them from the snares of the enemy.

Thus have ye made the commandment of God of none effect by your tradition. Ye hypocrites, well did Esaias prophesy of you, saying, This people draweth nigh unto me with their mouth, and honoureth me with their lips; but their heart is far from me. But in vain they do worship me, teaching for doctrines the commandments of men – Matthew 15:6-9 (KJV)

Jezebel does not want genuine prophetic worship under the direction of the Holy Spirit to go forth. She does not like free flowing services where people participate. Rather, she will institute an order of service that has scheduled activities.

Jezebel prefers an entertainment style environment of worship that keeps saints bewitched and emotionally charged. Jezebel easily deceives by working on their emotions. The more people or a church drifts towards emotionalism, sensationalism, and entertainment, the more Jezebel has room to operate. Many churches are known for their praise teams and choirs singing the latest in gospel music. Much of this is centered on tradition and not the Spirit of the Lord.

Now the Lord is that Spirit: and where the Spirit of the Lord is, there is liberty - 2 Corinthians 3:17 (KJV)

It is without question that when there is no liberty and freedom, or where the Holy Spirit does not have free range of motion, a Jezebel stronghold has been established.

Jezebel is a Pharisaical spirit that is obsessed with rules and rituals. The Pharisees loved their traditions and followed elaborate rituals to keep themselves set apart. In fact, the word Pharisee actually means separated. Jezebel will look to have "Christians" separate from others in the body of Christ based on denomination and race. Additionally, she will have churches develop mindsets that teach believers to stay away from sinners. This is in direct contrast to the word of God but fits nicely into Jezebels religious network.

The more religious a church is, the more witchcraft will prevail within it. Religious bishops, pastors and other leaders partner with Jezebel and protect her witchcraft from being exposed by releasing a spirit of fear among the flock. Watch for leaders and churches that impose heavy religious yokes on the people, specifically in the area of giving. A remark from the pulpit such as: "if you do not tithe, then you are cursed," is and example of religious control through fear.

Jezebel is a thief and a robber that steals from people through religious manipulation and prophetic witchcraft. In John chapter 10 Jesus said:

"All that ever came before me are thieves and robbers: but the sheep did not hear them. I am the door: by me if any man enter in, he shall be saved, and shall go in and out, and find pasture. The thief cometh not, but for to steal, and to kill, and to destroy: I am come that they might have life, and that they might have it more abundantly" – John 10: 8-10 (KJV)

This is not speaking about the devil as many assume. In

context, this is speaking about one who climbs up another way.

"He that entereth not by the door into the sheepfold, but climbeth up some other way, the same is a thief and a robber" – John 10:1 (KJV)

The term *"some other way"* is speaking expressly about the blind religious Pharisees that cast heavy burdens on people. This term and the use of the words *"thief and robber"* is a metaphor aimed at the religious system. We know this system today as Jezebel's Network.

To spin her web effectively, Jezebel will elevate her status by taking positions in the church in order to infect it with her witchcrafts. As a copycat demon, Jezebel has the ability to imitate and masquerade as someone that is highly anointed and operates in the gifts of the Spirit. Jezebel is skilled in exquisite spiritual vernacular and will have the host pray prayers against her. This augments her ability to remain undetected, specifically among religious organizations and people as their spiritual discernment is marred by their desire for connectivity to the religious culture.

Witchcraft is more common in the church than the average leader understands. It is primarily released through words, and Jezebel is slaughtering ministries by releasing word curses and casting spells on them. As Jezebel wiggles herself into positions of the leadership teams, she will initiate a campaign of accusations against others on the team. Accusation is a fundamental weapon of Jezebel that gets its momentum from religion. The religious Pharisees of the 1st century were constantly looking to accuse Jesus. In like manner, the religious spirit deployed by Jezebel will look to assassinate genuine apostolic and prophetic leaders and ministry.

Jezebel will have religious people look more at outward appearance. As such, they have a propensity to exalt the flesh and suppress the spirit.

The flesh

Now the doings (practices) of the flesh are clear (obvious):they are immorality, impurity, indecency, Idolatry, sorcery, enmity, strife, jealousy, anger (ill temper), selfishness, divisions (dissensions), party spirit (factions, sects with peculiar opinions, heresies), Envy, drunkenness, carousing, and the like. I warn you beforehand, just as I did previously, that those who do such things shall not inherit the kingdom of God – Galatians 5:19-21 (Amplified Bible)

One of the goals of Jezebel is to create a controlling network or web that gets you to focus on you! Be careful for those that do not want to serve the Lord but rather the flesh. Many people are consumed with themselves. Jezebel feasts on those that have a worldly mindset and trust in their own strength. The carnal nature is no match for Jezebel.

Many believers walk around like spiritual zombies. Zombies desire flesh. They're flesh eaters that feed off the intellect and emotions. The flesh is a way of thinking. It is a mindset that is patterned after the old man. The old man is the sin nature.

Zombies feed off the living and try to convert them. Beware of spiritual zombies that walk in the flesh. They are infamous of harboring the Jezebel spirit.

When Jezebel has her back to the wall and is near exposure, she will attempt to charm those around her by getting them to yield to the flesh and condone her actions. In the book of 2 Kings, Jezebel recognized she was in trouble when she got word that Jehu was coming. She sought to protect her interests through charming Jehu by her appearance. Jezebel put on makeup and styled her hair when she heard that Jehu was approaching. Her intention was to seduce him into becoming an collaborator through appealing to his flesh.

And when Jehu was come to Jezreel, Jezebel heard of it; and she painted her face, and tired her head, and looked out at a window – 2 Kings 9:30 (KJV)

People that do not renew their minds with the Word of God and satisfy the cravings of the flesh are targets and suspects when it comes to harboring Jezebel. Believers that are double-minded and do not seek the Kingdom of God are unstable souls. Serving God and the Flesh is spiritual schizophrenia. You cannot serve the carnal mind and the mind of the spirit. That which is Spirit is Spirit and that which is Flesh is Flesh.

For they that are after the flesh do mind the things of the flesh; but they that are after the Spirit the things of the Spirit. For to be carnally minded is death; but to be spiritually minded is life and peace. Because the carnal mind is enmity against God: for it is not subject to the law of God, neither indeed can

be. *So then they that are in the flesh cannot please God –
Romans 8:5-8 (KJV)*

Jezebel attacks and subsequently uses unstable souls.

*Having eyes full of adultery, and that cannot cease from sin;
beguiling unstable souls .... – 2 Peter 2:14 (KJV)*

When the mind is not renewed it becomes and open door for the lies and deceptions of Jezebel. When emotions are uncontrolled or remain in an undelivered state, Jezebel will seduce her prey into her bed of perversion. When the will does not desire the righteousness of God, Jezebel will commit fornication with God's servants.

The instability of one's soul (mind, will and emotions) provides a safe haven for Jezebel.

Perversion and Idolatry

Jezebel gains access through the lusts of the flesh. Individuals that engage in fornication, homosexuality, lesbianism, pornography and chronic masturbation (uncleanliness) will ultimately harbor the Jezebel or Ahab spirit. Those that idol people and things such as their home, car, education, culture (race), religious or political leader are partners in Jezebels witchcrafts.

Rebellion

Jezebel spirits are interwoven and connected with many

spirits; but one of the main spirits she partners with which is often overlooked is rebellion. Rebellion is the sin of witchcraft. Witchcraft is a work of the flesh.

The flesh is diametrically opposed to the Kingdom of Heaven. The Kingdom is the rule, reign authority and dominion of God. Therefore, the flesh resists the Kingdom and is rebellious to the King Himself. When a believer is walking in the flesh they are operating in witchcraft. Witchcraft is Rebellion (ref: *I Samuel 15:23*).

Those that are rebellious to law of the Lord and the governments (authorities) that are over them, harbor Jezebel.

But chiefly them that walk after the flesh in the lust of uncleanness, and despise government ...... – 2 Peter 2:10 (KJV)

Jezebel hates anyone placed in authority over her and will deliberately disrespect them by exalting her will over theirs.

When a person hosts the Jezebel spirit they are operating in rebellion (witchcraft). Rebellious people will typically lash out against authorities by indiscriminately bringing accusations against them in an attempt to gain sympathizers and cause division. Never become sympathetic to Jezebel or lenient towards the host. They must be treated as someone who lives in disobedience, and marked (identified), as such. The Jezebelic host must be quarantined and avoided by the congregation. You cannot act as though nothing is wrong. She must be confronted by the set-leaders of the ministry.

Perfectionism

Perfectionism is another common characteristic of a Jezebelic host. I've found that many Jezebelic hosts are anal-retentive in nature and feel the need to be in control of all aspects of his or her surroundings. Perfectionism is different than operating with a spirit of excellence. As ambassadors of the Kingdom of God, we should operate with highest quality and standards of excellence. But Jezebel uses perfectionism as a means to control, devalue and criticize. She is never satisfied and will become argumentative when it's not done her way. The truth is nobody is perfect and Jezebel will use criticism as a weapon to coast her victims into severe bondage.

Criticism

Criticism is a form of cursing, both of the person being criticized and of God. Jezebel is an enemy of God and Man and is a master of criticism. She likes to criticize everything. Jezebel needs to look better than everyone else and will criticize anyone who makes a suggestion or produces a plan.

Typically targeting a person with a wounded soul, Jezebel will deliberately criticize in an effort to punish and bring them back into subjection and under her control. Jezebel will not permit independence and uses criticism as a means to keep her host bound for decades.

Many adults are in need of deliverance due to Jezebelic parents and spouses that threw a massive array of missiles of criticism at them. Rejection, inferiority, fear and anger are some of the feelings people experience when someone they love and admire has told them that they "do not measure up." Watch and remain guarded against people that will not complement you. People that do not have anything positive and uplifting to say about you may be in the infancy stages of developing a Jezebel spirit.

When confronting someone about their criticism, Jezebel will instruct the host to pass it off as their nature or personality. Be alarmed if you hear the statement, "I'm critical of myself also." This is a plot of Jezebel to get you to understand and accept her manifestations. A critical nature is not a fruit of the spirit but rather a fruit of the flesh.

Also, watch for those that consistently point out all that's wrong with a person or organization. Jezebel will focus on all the shortcomings of others to draw attention away from her. She will be highly critical of others gifts, talents, office or anointing. Most of this will be camouflaged as a legitimate concern for the well being of the person or organization.

Jezebel has a sense of entitlement and demands compliance to her unrealistic expectations. When she does not get her way she will become very critical of those around her.

Jealousy

At times, criticism can lock arms with the spirit of Jealousy. One of the works of the flesh is Jealousy. It brings in envy, malice and hatred. A person that is jealous of others will harbor the spirit of Jezebel. Jezebel will most likely use a high-profile type person that is exceptionally extroverted, opinionated and highly visible. Watch for signs of violence, rage and fierce indignation.

Discord and Division

There are some people that love to debate and argue about everything. They are typically controllers that cause strife, division and disunity. Jezebel uses this work of the flesh as a tool to bring in confusion and turmoil. These are troublemakers that empower and enable Jezebel to work in their life. They are deceived and blind to the fact that they are operating in witchcraft and harboring the Jezebel network.

Sounding board

Most churches and ministries want to "counsel" out demons. This is a waste of time and further plays into the Jezebelic network strategy. Jezebel must be cast out of the host and her network must be dismantled from the organization or family. Counseling programs do nothing more than provide Jezebel the platform to manifest and release her curses. She will run circles around the average Christian counselor that wants the host to "talk about their problems." Further, once you have been identified as a sounding board for Jezebel, I can almost guarantee you that she will bring you into submission to her network by draining you of energy.

Have you ever been on the phone with a person for hours as they tell you about all their problems and issues? Isn't it amazing that after hearing them out, two things typically occur? The first thing is that you feel extremely exhausted and drained. A sharp pain behind your eyes can even accompany this feeling of being drained of energy. The second things is once the conversation is over, you may experience the feeling that you need to fix the problem. This is classic Jezebel.

Those who are needy, talkative and constantly wanting to get into your ear are harboring the Jezebel spirit.

Leeches

The horseleech hath two daughters, crying, Give, give. There are three things that are never satisfied, yea, four things say not, It is enough – Proverbs 30:15 (KJV)

Have you ever been around a person that is always looking to get something? Perhaps you're a person that is always in need and has an entitlement mindset that you're owed something. If so, you're aligning yourself with the spirit of Jezebel.

The horseleech has two daughters that cry out "Give, Give!" They never get enough. The more you give them, the more they want.

Jezebel works through her host to suck from others. She will deplete you of your energy, time and resources. She uses her manipulative capabilities to wear your resistance down so you will agree to her demands. If you've ever felt as if it's your responsibility to fix someone else's problem after they talked to you, then Jezebel is in operation. Be extra careful you're not being set up to harbor the spirit yourself.

Here's a word that you must learn to say………….. No!

It's much wiser to start off with a "no" than a yes. It's easier to change "no" into "yes," but it's extremely difficult to turn a "yes" into "no."

Practice it now:

- Can I have gas money? …….. No!
- Can you pick me up for work? …….. No!
- Can I stay at your house? ……. No!
- Can I talk to you about something? (Emphatically) No!
- Can you pay for my conference fee …… No way!

Breaking free from Jezebel's web requires repentance and many encounters with pure deliverance ministry. Deliverance ministry is not for the lazy Christian who walks in the flesh and wants nothing more than a religious one-hour of power service or a simple prayer released over them. It's for the humble and teachable. It's for those that have a desire for the Kingdom of God and the Spirit filled life rather than an appetite for the flesh.

Jezebel must be addressed. To many have been wounded from Jezebelic activities. Church leaders must be relentless in their quest for genuine deliverance programs to be established in their churches. If you don't know how to root demons out and dismantle Jezebel's network, contact the experts. Ask for help.

Be very skeptical of flaky deliverance that uses a mystical approach and melodramatic Hollywood performances. Stay clear of esoteric methods that give Jezebel a platform to cut-up.

Remember, Elijah was Jezebel's enemy, but it took Jehu to bring an end to Jezebel. Jehu would not rest until Jezebel was dead. He was on assignment to eradicate witchcraft and whoredoms from the land. Jehu was a man of war. You must aggressively attack Jezebel without with a combative and militant attitude. Confrontation is the key. Don't play with Jezebel.

And when Jehu was come to Jezreel, Jezebel heard of it; and she painted her face, and tired her head, and looked out at a window. And as Jehu entered in at the gate, she said, Had Zimri peace, who slew his master? And he lifted up his face to the window, and said, Who is on my side? who? And there looked out to him two or three eunuchs. And he said, Throw her down. So they threw her down: and some of her blood was sprinkled on the wall, and on the horses: and he trode her under foot. And when he was come in, he did eat and drink, and said, Go, see now this cursed woman, and bury her: for she is a king's daughter. And they went to bury her: but they found no more of her than the skull, and the feet, and the palms of her hands. Wherefore they came again, and told him. And he said, This is the word of the Lord, which he spake by his servant Elijah the Tishbite, saying, In the portion of Jezreel shall dogs eat the flesh of Jezebel: And the carcase of Jezebel shall be as dung upon the face of the field in the portion of Jezreel; so that they shall not say, This is Jezebel – 2 Kings 9:30-37 (KJV)

Effective leaders will not ignore conflict. They embrace it and therefore will expose Jezebel's network. They go hard after her eunuchs. Within a church, the Jezebel host must be removed from his or her position of authority by the set-leader. This could be the pastor or an apostle, but clearly it should be by the one in authority and not others. This holds true for the family. The male-man needs to address this spirit. Sorry men, it's time to get out of your cave and take back your family.

Jezebel is a strong warring spirit. If you are not properly trained in spiritual warfare, and don't comprehend the authority you have in Christ, stand down.

Additionally, never seek to rule over Jezebel until you are first submitting to Kingdom rule over your own life. Jezebel knows the real from the counterfeit. If you cannot submit to God and His authorities, Jezzy will run circles around you.

I've found that preaching the gospel of the Kingdom in a bold non-conforming way will agitate the network. Begin to expose the host that is harboring the fugitive called Jezebel. Once you do, the authority of the network will quickly dissolve and either the host will repent and get free, or run from the one that has the real authority from God.

And I gave her space to repent of her fornication; and she repented not. Behold, I will cast her into a bed, and them that commit adultery with her into great tribulation, except they repent of their deeds. And I will kill her children with death; and all the churches shall know that I am he which searcheth the reins and hearts: and I will give unto every one of you according to your works – Revelations 2:21-23 (KJV)

Jezebel networks are capable of doing severe damage and typically result in splits, divisions and discord. Once the gospel of the kingdom of God exposes the evil works of darkness lurking within a church, Jezebel will begin to work at an accelerated pace to bring sabotage to the ministry and gather her children for their departure. Because Jezebel will not repent, her only route she has is to escape from that which exposed her.

Chapter Four

After-Shock

Because of its networking nature, when you attack Jezebel, you will get hit unexpectedly from all sides as Jezebel sends signals throughout the network. I call this "the aftershock."

An aftershock is the repercussion of going through the intense battle against Jezebel's network.

Shortly after her departure, Jezebel's sorceries begin to noticeably rise to the surface. Constant confusion, unexplained illnesses, financial troubles, anger and depression are only a few of the signatures left behind. It's as if she left a time bomb that is synchronize to explode at the same time in everyone's life. Although the host has been delivered or decided to leave the church or ministry, her web is full of toxic waste that is designed to cause her victims to self-destruct.

The aftermath from the departure of the spirit of Jezebel is no less dramatic and disturbing to her intended prey. Jezebel's web of entanglement extends to virtually every person the host had interaction with. Once the parties that hosted the spirit of Jezebel leave the church or ministry there is residual toxic waste that needs to be flushed out.

Jezebel is a Black Widow spider spirit that lures her intended victims into her web of destruction. Once Jezebel inserts her fangs deep into the minds of people and releases her toxic venom, they become paralyzed and ultimately have the life sucked out of them. This is referred to as the "black widow spider syndrome." This term is used as black widow spiders devour their mates after engaging in intercourse with them. The black widow spider's venomous neurotoxin leaves it victims entangled in the web.

These victims remain stuck in a spiritual web full of dead prey. Jezebel will always leave this toxic web of witchcraft that if left un-addressed it could potentially lead to additional causalities of war. It is strongly recommended that a solid round of deliverance take place immediately after any manifestation and departure of the Jezebel spirit.

Jezebel's aftershock is a massive array of witchcraft tactics that are intentionally targeted at the ministry; it's leaders and team members. Word curses, prophetic sorcery and psychic prayers are some of the ways this witchcraft is released.

I recall a time when a Queen Jezebel and some of her children were exposed. They were given an opportunity to repent but would not and ended up leaving the ministry. After the initial relief of eradicating this spirit, over the next few days I began to experience feelings of depression, fatigue and weariness. Additionally a strong spirit of accusation arose in the ministry. Affected legacy people began to falsely accuse other believers of talking about them. Distrust, insecurity and fear are some of the things that began to grip the people.

Remember, Jezebel employs the craft of witches in her arsenal of weaponry. Those that have been victimized by the spirit of witchcraft typically will not know they are under attack.

It will require outside sources or other intermediaries to bring exposure to the spirit of witchcraft in operation. Some of the feelings you may experience when a spirit of witchcraft has been release against you are:

- The need to be unattached, distanced and isolated from:
    - The Body of Christ
    - Friends
    - Family
    - Leaders / those in authority
    - Those that speak truth to you
- Fear / Phobia
    - That others are talking about you
- Insecurity / Inferiority
- Rejection
- Bitterness
- Loss of Joy
- Slothful & Lazy
- Anger
- Frustrated
- Intolerant of others / irritable
- Anxiety
- Worry
- Trouble sleeping

What about the hosts and the eunuchs?

Those that were bound by this evil spirit either as the Queen Jezebel or served in her bedchamber had one of two paths they could have gone down. They may have repented and received deliverance or resisted and fled to another ministry. (Please note, in the event of a marriage, the host may have left their spouse for another person).

In addition to destroying those around her, Jezebel especially hates the host she was controlling. One of the missions of Jezebel is to kill the prophets. Victims that harbored the Jezebel spirit are often anointed themselves in the prophetic or worship arena.

Jezebel will release a fury of rage and retaliation against the ministry and restored hosts. Jezebel will typically torment those that were exposed and moved on to other ministries or relationships. This vengeance can be so acute that it renders the person bound with severe spiritual schizophrenia and delusion.

The following are some of the major attacks I've experienced in my fight against Jezebel & Ahab.

Retaliation

Anytime you preach the good news of the Kingdom of God and give people the truth it will challenge them. The word of God is truth.

Sanctify them through thy truth: thy word is truth – John 17:17 (KJV)

Knowing truth is what makes people free.

And ye shall know the truth, and the truth shall make you free – John 8:32 (KJV)

When truth is given to people it shines the light of the word of God into the dark places that exist in their life. Jezebel, her evil network and wicked sorceries prefer the darkness. She wants to remain hidden so she can deceive the host into believing their thoughts and actions are correct. But when truth is released it will expose sin and demand repentance. Jezebel hates repentance and she hates the voice the cries loud for it. She will look to slander, discredit, defame, discourage and make fearful the one with the message of truth.

John the Baptist preached a message of repentance and the coming Kingdom.

In those days came John the Baptist, preaching in the wilderness of Judaea, And saying, Repent ye: for the kingdom of heaven is at hand – Matthew 3:1-2 (KJV)

John preached the truth and exposed the sin of King Herod. His wife Herodias was married to him unlawfully. John spoke truth about their perverted relationship.

For John had said unto Herod, It is not lawful for thee to have thy brother's wife – Mark 6:18 (KJV)

Herodias was related by marriage to a Jewish High Priest who was the father of Herod's third wife. It was against Jewish law to marry another man while one's husband was still alive. The only exception to this law is in the case of adultery when the marriage covenant is violated.

Despite Herod's displeasure with John preaching against this relationship, he was afraid to kill John because he was a mighty prophet that was held in high esteem by the people. However, Herodias wanted him dead.

Herodias harbored the spirit of Jezebel. Her perversions and actions are classic Jezebelic nature. She became highly agitated at John the Baptist when he exposed her and her (Ahab) husband Herod.

And Herodias was angry (enraged) with him and held a grudge against him and wanted to kill him; but she could not – Mark 6:19 (Amplified Bible)

Herodias (Jezebel) devised a very well thought out retaliatory plan against John. Jezebel spirits are very meticulous and will set up traps by enlisting the help of Ahab and her children. In this case, Herodias (Jezebel) used her unsuspecting husband Herod (Ahab) and daughter Salome. The plan was to use the perverted dance of Herod's stepdaughter Salome to entertain him and bring him to a point of ecstasy.

But when Herod's birthday was kept, the daughter of Herodias danced before them, and pleased Herod. Whereupon he promised with an oath to give her whatsoever she would ask. And she, being before instructed of her mother, said, Give me here John Baptist's head in a charger – Matthew 14:6-8 (KJV)

The diabolical plan worked. Herodias vengeful fury of retaliation came down heavily and the prophets' head was severed.

And he sent, and beheaded John in the prison. And his head was brought in a charger, and given to the damsel: and she brought it to her mother - Matthew 14:10-11

The seduction of Salome's dance that led to the beheading of John the Baptist was none other than a Jezebel spirit. This spirit seeks to kill those that expose Jezebel and releases the truth.

Jezebel's retaliation works in many ways. In some cases it will be forceful and immediate. In others, it may be slow and progressive. Regardless, when it surfaces it must be addressed quickly. It cannot be viewed as simply an anomaly but rather as part of Jezebels toxic afterbirth.

Sabotage

Jezebel will sabotage ministry. When confronted, exposed and rooted out her demonic spores of witchcraft will be activated. Jezebel is a terrorist spirit that strategically places bombs, set to detonate at various times after her departure. She was able to accomplish this because most likely she was given a position of leadership and acquired private information. The bottom line is, she was trusted. When you place your trust in someone there is a propensity not to watch over him or her. You believe their words and do not question their loyalty. Jezebel uses this to her advantage.

Covenant breaking

One of the ways she will sabotage is through broken promises. Covenant breaking is a powerful weapon of Jezebel.

Jezebel, together with her children, labored feverishly to get in position where they could monopolize entire areas of ministry. Jezebel will verbally commit to being responsible for critical components of a project. She wants you to depend on the controlling network she has meticulously manufactured. When exposed, she will depart the ministry in an abrupt manner, taking with her those that committed adultery with her. This may include entire departments, specifically musicians, praise teams, dancers, intercessory prayer teams, cell groups or support and common interest groups.

Jezebelic hosts will damage, disrupt and impair internet access, sound and media equipment, musical equipment, intentionally lose files, delete files and lose critical data (passwords). She will install viruses on computers, break equipment, and vandalize property.

Discrediting

Similar to the saboteurs Tobiah and Sanballat in the book of Nehemiah, Jezebel speaks against the purposes and plans of God. Through words, she attacks that which God is seeking to establish and build in the earth. Jezebels words of discord, criticism and mockery are designed to tear down and destroy others instead of giving encouragement.

When Sanballat heard that we were rebuilding the wall he exploded in anger, vilifying the Jews. In the company of his Samaritan cronies and military he let loose: "What are these miserable Jews doing? Do they think they can get everything back to normal overnight? Make building stones out of make–

believe?" At his side, Tobiah the Ammonite jumped in and said, "That's right! What do they think they're building? Why, if a fox climbed that wall, it would fall to pieces under his weight - Nehemiah 4:1-3 (Message bible)

With the departure of the Jezebel queen, watch for signs of people doubting the vision of leadership and the organization. Jezebel seeks to discredit and find imperfections in authority so that their leadership has no credibility and their words have no power. Remember, Jezebel wants to reestablish her web of control and will attempt to do so through sabotage.

Jezebel will always look to discredit what you're building. Jezebelic hosts that left the ministry will quickly move to other churches or networks to release an arsenal of lies against you. This is designed to assassinate your character and keep you from advancing in life. Jezebel will attempt to demonize you to your friends, your church or family members.

Jezebel will look to sabotage you through the use of social media distribution channels. In most cases, the Jezebel host that was exposed will immediately un-friend and block you on Facebook and Twitter. This is designed so that you do not see her accusations and indiscriminate targeted assaults against you.

At times, Jezebel may enable you to hear or read about an accusation against you. This tactic is used to lure you into a carnal battle with her. Don't take the bait and respond by using fleshly retaliatory methods. Never mock or use sarcasm against her. Do not let her drag you into an argument. Rather, expose the works of darkness through being an example of Godly character and bearer of truth.

Take no part in and have no fellowship with the fruitless deeds and enterprises of darkness, but instead [let your lives be so in contrast as to] expose and reprove and convict them – Ephesians 5:11 (Amplified Version)

Always treat the host as someone who lives in disobedience. Do not be tolerant of her association with witchcraft. Stay focused and speak the Word of God only regarding the matter.

Leaders must be extra careful and not succumb to this trickery. After a long battle with Jezebel and her network, leaders can become weary, fatigued and depressed. At times, leaders may find themselves questioning their own beliefs, calling and commitment even to the point of wanting to throw in the towel.

Giving up is the greatest threat to your success when battling Jezebel. She will wear you down, mentally, emotionally and physically. Don't give up! You have the victory.

Finances impaired

Jezebel's aftershock will reverberate and sabotage finances.

When believers are unable to give at a high capacity it could be due to the residual witchcraft of Jezebel's network. The Jezebel spirit will castrate believers and turn them into eunuch's causing their giving (seed) to stop. Jezebel does not want people to be blessed and withholding seed will prevent increase in the financial arena.

When Jezebel and her network is challenged, she will direct the host to stop giving in anticipation that you as a leader will soften your battle against this ancient warlord. A Jehu anointing is required to command this network to break up and liberate the eunuchs.

If Jezebel cannot influence you to stop giving in the Kingdom she will come at you in another direction. Mysterious and unusual expenses may surface that is designed to hinder cash flow.

Additionally strange accidents and unexplained illnesses requiring medical attention are indicators of witchcraft assignments against you. Jezebel attempts to squeeze you through attacks against your finances. She will employ the spirit of Python to restrict the flow of money and resources into your ministry, family and business. However, do not fret. Once identified simply exercise dominion and authority over her and she will be forced to cease from her debauchery against you and your finances will increase.

Jezebel's witchcrafts will also look to cast a poverty mindset on entire churches, families and organizations. Once Jezebel is exposed and her direct control is eliminated, she will cast a spell of lack and poverty on that which opposed her. Be on guard against the spirit of fear that aggressively attacks the soul to get you to embrace poverty and lack. This is designed to get one to stop growing, building, investing and obtaining wealth.

Financial sabotage is usually carried out in a covert and indirect manner. However, there may be cases of harsh sabotage such as car accidents, burglary, destruction of property and job loss.

Accusation

This is one of the Jezebel networks most lethal shockwaves after it's departure – accusation. I've seen this spirit employed by Jezebel bring fear, confusion, torment, anger and bitterness into ministries and marriages. A spirit of accusation can split churches, separate marriages and break up families.

When Jezebel provokes people to release indiscriminate accusations and blame others for why something occurred they might become very lethargic and extremely passive in the vision. This accusation spirit can also bring people under control.

The spirit of accusation forms partnerships with the religious spirit and the flesh. This three-fold cord becomes a powerful whip that Jezebel uses to beat down her victims.

When accusing others one looks to find faults in others so that they can handle their own compromises and negligence.

The spirit of accusation can make a person see the faults in others, specifically the church and its leadership, or in a marriage, their spouse. Jezebel is affluent in making the faults in the church the central issue. This will often lead to the devaluing of the importance of belonging to a church for spiritual enrichment, edification and development.

If a spirit of accusation is able to make a person accuse others, that person will find it very hard to forgive. The spirit of accusation works hard to get you to operate in un-forgiveness. Un-forgiveness leads to bitterness. The root of bitterness is a toxic poison that goes deep into the soul and ultimately affects the body.

Repent therefore of this thy wickedness, and pray God, if perhaps the thought of thine heart may be forgiven thee. For I perceive that thou art in the gall of bitterness, and in the bond of iniquity – Acts 8:22-23 (KJV)

Jezebel will not only work on you to accuse others, but also to accuse you to yourself. Accusing spirits' seek to separate us from God, others and ourselves. Satan uses an old military tactic of "divide and conquer."

I have also found that Jezebel will bring accusations against the saints through Facebook and other broad-based social media outlets. Her method here is double-sided. On one hand she will look to have those who have been wounded by Jezebel to release indiscriminate posts about Jezebel in an attempt to bring about much collateral damage. On the other hand, Jezebel will lie to numerous people in an attempt to get them to believe that the person, who wrote about the Jezebel spirit in a general sense, is talking about them.

Jezebel will accuse the Pastor and leaders to their congregations. She will lie to people by telling them "that sermon was about you" or "the pastor no longer loves you."

Jezebel's fury of accusation doesn't stop here. Crazy dreams where individuals experience thoughts that leadership or the Pastor no longer likes them and is going to ask them to leave the church have been reported. Others have gone through and experienced fear, phobias and anxiety attacks.

Pastors and leaders who seek to deal with the Jezebel spirit should be aware of operating in an accusing spirit. If a pastor or leader brings a charge against a Jezebelite, it must be based on factual evidence supported by witnesses. Accusations that are based solely on assumptions or what you believe is going on, are extremely dangerous. Many improper accusations that are fueled by fear and suspicion only result in retaliation against the Pastor and the churches leadership.

Jezebel is a seducing spirit that looks to lure you into a retaliatory posture shortly after her bombardment of false accusations against you. Never publicly criticize, mock or launch accusations against the person hosting the Jezebel spirit. Rather the host must submit to authority and brought to a place of genuine repentance. The Jezebel spirit must be exposed for her witchcrafts and confronted at all levels.

Finally, when Jezebel accuses you, do not stay silent or simply pray about it. Instead, rebut everything she says, directly to her face. If she accused you publicly, demand that a public apology be made. Truthful communication is a key in crushing Jezebels network.

Physical effects

Two of the most common symptoms when being attacked by witchcraft are headaches and fatigue. Severe headaches or pressure on the brain that renders one confused is a sign that witchcraft has been released. Fatigue is a leading indicator that the demonic weapon of witchcraft is operating against you. Witchcraft drains the energy and life right out of you. If, after the Jezebelic host leaves, one begins to feels exhausted, depressed, fatigued and drained, there is likely a remnant of her web that must be addressed.

Other symptoms can include confusion, memory loss, loss of identity, weariness, a draining feeling, depression, wanting to give up, the feeling to run (i.e. Elijah), or lack of a sense of accomplishment etc.

Finally, Jezebel is the premier "Back-stabber". Watch for sharp pains in the neck, lower back and sides after confronting this evil warlord. I've seen situations where demons have nested in the spine of individuals after a bout with Jezebel.

Stress

Once Jezebel is located, exposed and dealt with, the ministry will be under a whirlwind of chaos and pressure. New issues will develop and will be used as ammunition to deflect from dismantling the web and killing her afterbirth. To lure you away from taking out her entire network, she will bombard you with stress. To understand this more fully we need only look at the life of Elijah.

After having a successful campaign where he defeated the prophets of Baal on Mount Carmel, Elijah felt the full concussion of Jezebel's aftershock.

Ahab told Jezebel all that Elijah had done and how he had slain all the prophets [of Baal] with the sword. Then Jezebel sent a messenger to Elijah, saying, So let the gods do to me, and more also, if I make not your life as the life of one of them by this time tomorrow. Then he was afraid and arose and went for his life and came to Beersheba of Judah [over eighty miles, and out of Jezebel's realm] and left his servant there. But he himself went a day's journey into the wilderness and came and sat down under a lone broom or juniper tree and asked that he might die. He said, It is enough; now, O Lord, take away my life; for I am no better than my fathers – I Kings 19:1-4 (Amplified Version)

Immediately after this great victory, Jezebel threatened to kill Elijah. Clearly he was in a stressful situation. What did he do? Elijah freaked-out, and ran for his life. Jezebel's threats and witchcrafts will deplete you of all of your physical strength and will mentally fatigue you.

Fighting Ahab, Jezebel, her network and demonic spawn can stress you out. Watch for signs of intense pressure where you feel as though your body and mind cannot handle any more stress. Depression, isolation, thoughts of giving up, potentially even suicidal thoughts after a victorious battle against Jezebel are extremely dangerous. It's very important that you surround yourself with mature prophetic believers whom will speak into your life and strengthen you.

Sickness, the economy, broken relationships, marital problems, overweight, crime, racism, children, jobs and careers are some of the vehicles Jezebel will use to stress you out.

Signs of Jezebel induced stress

- You're exhausted for no apparent reason
- You gain weight rapidly
- Have a difficult time waking up after 8 hours of sleep
- Consistent or chronic colds, flu and sinus infections
- Feel overwhelmed
- Have panic or anxiety attacks
- Lack concentration
- Crave junk food consistently, especially high sugar and salt content
- Crave caffeine, sodas or "Red bull" drinks as stimulants
- Heavy or irregular menstrual cycles
- Reduced or no sex drive
- Poor Digestion (bloating, chronic gas and poor bowel movements)
- Insomnia
- Skin issues (itching and pigmentation problems)
- Fibromyalgia
- Thyroid issues (Hyper)
- Chronic fatigue syndrome
- Arthritis
- Inflammatory diseases

Fatigue

One of the consequences of a Jezebelic attack on your life is fatigue. Jezebel is a witch that will release her craft of sorcery by attacking the mind and emotions. Weariness, extreme tiredness and the constant feeling of being drained are clear indications of her Demonic assault. No amount of vitamins, sleep or exercise can counter this divination. Jezebel must be rooted out through genuine deliverance ministry.

The aftermath of contending with the Jezebel spirit will exhaust you. You may find yourself sleeping 10-12 hours per day and yet wake up exhausted. You may feel as if all of the energy has been sucked out from you. Be very careful that you do not permit this aftershock to keep you from work, praying and fulfilling your commitments. Jezebel wants to stir up trouble in your life and one of the ways she does it is through fatigue.

Often, after a great victory over Jezebel you may become physically and emotionally susceptible to fatigue and fear.

Elijah had this aftershock attack from Jezebel just after he experienced an amazing spiritual victory where he confronted Ahab, called down fire from heaven, and destroyed the prophets of Baal. He did all of this in the power of the Spirit. After the confrontation between Elijah and the prophets of Baal, Ahab told Jezebel what happened to her prophets. After hearing about their annihilation, Jezebel sent word to Elijah that she had taken a vow to kill him. Then we see what Elijah did –

When Elijah saw how things were, he ran for dear life to Beersheba, far in the south of Judah. He left his young servant there and then went on into the desert another day's journey. He came to a lone broom bush and collapsed in its shade, wanting in the worst way to be done with it all—to just die: "Enough of this, God! Take my life—I'm ready to join my ancestors in the grave!" Exhausted, he fell asleep under the lone broom bush – I Kings 19:3-5 (the Message Bible)

Elijah was drained and exhausted. After his great victory he just doesn't have the energy to contend with Jezebel anymore. Many of us, like Elijah need to recognize that we are often vulnerable to her residual attacks after a spiritual victory. There may be times where you simply feel as if you want to run and hide. This is common, specifically when you thought the battle was over and then another assault from Jezebel suddenly appears.

Who is the Enabler?

As discussed in chapter 3, there can be no Jezebel or a network without an enabling Ahab. The real question is, who supported and enabled this evil witch to move about covertly and operate with full range of motion? Modern day pastors, leaders and husbands are infamous for taking a casual and a somewhat passive approach to confronting people, specifically women or wives when things are out of order.

1. Passive Pastors

Many Pastors and leaders want to be cute in ministry. They have an image to project and uphold. Many times they will delegate the management of issues to others or conduct nice warm counseling sessions with people. While counseling adds some value, you cannot counsel Jezebel out of a person. She must be contended with. Pastors and church leaders that do not address the spirit of Jezebel operating in their churches are enablers. The leadership at the church in Thyatira in the 1st century was rebuked for their tolerance of the Jezebel spirit.

And to the angel (messenger) of the assembly (church) in Thyatira write: These are the words of the Son of God, Who has eyes that flash like a flame of fire, and Whose feet glow like bright and burnished and white- hot bronze: I know your record and what you are doing, your love and faith and service and patient endurance, and that your recent works are more numerous and greater than your first ones. But I have this against you: that you tolerate the woman Jezebel, who calls herself a prophetess [claiming to be inspired], and who is teaching and leading astray my servants and beguiling them into practicing sexual vice and eating food sacrificed to idols. – Revelation 2:18-20 (Amplified Version)

Pastors have a responsibility to contend with this spirit. Unfortunately today many Pastors have become more administratively focused on church business affairs then equipping the flock. Church growth (membership), building funds and activities are typically at the forefront of a churches vision. Additionally, many churches have been established on evangelical models rather than an apostolic model.

The church is built on the foundation of the apostles and prophets.

And are built upon the foundation of the apostles and prophets, Jesus Christ himself being the chief corner stone – Ephesians 2:20 (KJV)

The apostolic grace is designed to contend with evil spirits. Apostles challenge and resist Jezebel through their preaching, teaching, prophesying and deliverance ministries. Genuine apostolic ministry is a military type grace that is combative and aggressive against Jezebel's network. The apostolic model of ministry includes spiritual warfare and deliverance ministry. Traditional leaders, churches and denominations that have not been built on an apostolic model will be deficient in deliverance ministry and become a breeding ground for Jezebel networks.

Many Pastors and leaders are afraid to contend with Jezebel for fear of losing members. Leaders that are not confrontational are enablers to Jezebel.

Sometimes male Pastors may be reluctant to confront issues between two or more women. This could be due to the emotional element of women. Remember, Jezebel is a drama queen and will cry and accuse you of not being sympathetic or loving. I had one Jezebel accuse me of not being merciful and another one accuses me of not having a heart of a father. Of course this is an old witchcraft tactic designed to have a Pastor feel threatened and withdraw from confronting Jezebel.

You cannot back down from addressing this spirit. If so, you are enabling it!

2. Girly men

A Husband can be an enabler to a Jezebelic wife. Many men do not want to confront things because they simply want peace and quiet. Said a different way, they want their way. They're girly men that don't want conflict and therefore will tolerate this spirit by submitting to it.

In a marriage a Jezebelic wife will twists and turn situations and engage in long drawn out communication that wears down the husband. In a desperate attempt to end the matter, he will not address the issue at hand but rather simply say he's sorry. However, Jezebel will capitalize on this and refuse to "kiss and make up," leaving issues in an ongoing dispute.

If confronted, a Jezebel wife will become defensive and combative. She will swiftly respond with emotional drama or uncontrollable outbursts of crying and accuse you of attacking her. She will make you feel lost, defeated and completely confused. You are being emasculated and abused through her intimidations, guilt trips, control, and manipulation, and there is no peace.

………… How can peace exist as long as the fornications of your mother Jezebel and her witchcrafts are so many? – 2 Kings 9:22 (Amplified version)

Husbands stop being an enabler to Jezebel. Rise up and do something about your marriage and family. Be the man! Teach your wife the word of God. Remind her that she must submit to the authority God has given you as her husband. Take charge as the leader of your household as you are supposed to do as a man of God. You will no longer permit or tolerate any ungodly rebellious behavior in your home. Start to pray with your wife daily. Be bold in your prayers and command anything unclean to come out of her and you.

For the husband is the head of the wife, even as Christ is the head of the church – Ephesians 5:23 (KJV)

3. Waffling Women

Women the time has come to stand up and fight against the spirit of Jezebel operating in your husband or significant other. Stop vacillating and enabling Jezebel to operate in your husband.

Wives that have controlling husbands typically are Ahab wives that enable and in some cases encourage the Jezebelic behavior in the husband. Ladies its time to stop devaluing yourself and see yourselves as God created you – precious and valuable.

Jezebelic husbands are the byproduct of Jezebel parents. Whether it was his father or mother, Jezebel will always pass her spirit on to the next generation. Controlling men that physically, mentally and emotionally abuse women were raised in an environment of violence, sexual perversion and witchcraft.

Ahab women often marry to quickly without checking out the background of their potential spouse. Remember, Jezebel men want to marry their victims quickly. He is impulsive and wants his victims dependent on him. He portrays false integrity, appears helpful, comforting, generous and loving. Take your time before jumping into a relationship.

Ahab women do not see themselves as beautiful and intelligent but rather inferior to their Jezebel husbands. They have become slaves and servants rather than loving wives. Typically they have great ideas, even to the point of understanding career aspirations. Unfortunately, they shy away from ever accomplishing anything beyond being their husbands' personal maid and sex partner. Ahab wives are treated more as a concubine than a wife.

Additionally, Jezebel husbands can appear to be very spiritual. They will interpret scripture in a manner that is convenient to controlling their wife, rather than what God had in mind. Study the word of God together and properly interpret the scriptures.

Characteristics of Ahab type women

- Financially supports her Jezebelic husband or boyfriend
- Emotionally unstable
- Will not take responsibility for her problems
- Promiscuous and engages in perverted sex acts to be accepted
- Get's pregnant out of guilt
- Severely depressed
- Easily influenced by peers
- Sees herself as the reason she's abused
- Severely rejected
- Shame
- Inferiority complex

Women must take authority in the spirit and put an end to enabling the Jezebel spirit from operating in the home and marriage. Self-worth is critical as is proper understanding of the "King-Priest" dimension of a believer.

Women that are in positions of being an enabler must confront the spirit of Jezebel operating in their husbands. Let him know that you will no longer be abused on any level. Fast and pray in the spirit. Take dominion and engage in spiritual warfare.

Bonus - tips to keeping a Jezebel or Ahab man out of your life.

- Ladies beware of Jezebelic pimps that roam in churches with the sole purpose of finding a woman but not God
- Check out his past before you get involved with any man.
- Look at how he treats others, especially his mother. A sure sign of potential problems is when the man you're considering marrying does not treat his mother with respect, affection and love
- Don't hook up with men that have not hooked up with God.
- Cultivate relationships with those that add value to you, not take it from you.
- Beware of men that have more invested in their gym shoes and what's around their neck than they do in a bank account.
- If you do not value yourself, don't expect him to.
- Young Ladies, stop trying to be the next "pop star" and be the next genuine YOU. Men value originally, not cheap copies.
- Beware of men that never want to grow up but rather stay in a High School mentality.
- Beware of men the will not work.
- Ladies, stop seeing yourself with a broke "player" and start seeing your self with a man that has character, a job and a vision.

Finally ladies, to men there are two types of women - One you sleep with and the other type you marry. How you carry and present yourself by way you dress, talk, dance and the people you're around classifies yourself.

Chapter Five

Deliverance from Jezebel

The people needing help (the Jezebel host, the Jezebel target, the Jezebel suspect and Ahab enablers) will need to actively engage in deliverance ministry.

With the spirit of Jezebel running rampant in churches and families everywhere, there is clearly a tremendous need for deliverance ministry to be active in the lives of all believers. Many are coming into our churches seeking help with emotional issues and wounds that have built up over decades. Deliverance ministry is a present day ministry of the Lord Jesus Christ.

Remember, no one can be controlled unless they allow themselves to be controlled. The choice is yours. Your will is the key. Demons, Jezebel or Satan himself do not have the ability to overpower you. They must be given permission to gain access into your life.

To get free from the Jezebel Network here are some basic things you can do to start receiving deliverance from the Jezebel spirit.

1. Forgive

Choose to forgive others for what they did to you. Also, forgive yourself for responding in the manner you did. Make a decision not to blame yourself or others for what happened anymore. When we do not forgive, we are given over to the tormentors. The tormentors are demons spirits.

2. Repent

Confess and repent that you were either an enabler to Jezebel or harbored the spirit yourself. Repent of control and manipulation over others. Repent of witchcraft (rebellion), idolatry and admit you were wrong.

3. Break all Soul Ties with the network

Those entangled in this Black widow spider's web must repent and liberate themselves by breaking all soul ties with the Queen Jezebel and her associated demonic imps.

Cut the cord and remove yourself from bad or perverted relationships. This includes sex partners, common-law marriages, adulterous affairs, sexting with people, and fantasy lust.

There can also be soul ties between yourself and another person, without any sexual relationship involved.

4. Submit to authority

Submit to the authority God has placed in your life. Submit to your husband, observe the counsel of church elders, submit to your employer, obey the government, and submit to the Holy Spirit.

Submission to authority and obedience to God is critical.

5. Renunciation

Renounce is to disown, reject, leave and refuse something. Begin to renounce anger, rebellion, pride, hatred, jealousy, lust and accusations towards others. Renounce all relations with Jezebelic networks, allegiance to her will, alliances and agreements made through demonic people, places or things associated with her network.

Your renunciation can go something like this:

"I now renounce, break, sever and remove all unholy soul ties created between myself and _____ through the act of _____ in Jesus' name!"

Prayers against Jezebel

Father, in the name of Jesus I repent from being used as a host for the Jezebel spirit. I ask you to forgive me for my association with her network, eunuchs and children. I also repent of all idolatry, lusts of the flesh and areas of rebellion.

Jezebel, you are defeated. Every assignment against me, my family, my ministry, my children, my business and my church is canceled out, in Jesus name. I no longer fear you and you have no control over me.

Jezebel, I stand against you in the name of Jesus. It is written within the Word of God that whatsoever I bind on earth shall be bound in heaven and whatsoever I loose on earth shall be loosed in heaven. Therefore I bind up the ruling spirit of Jezebel in the unseen realm. I bind up Jezebel and I loose God's warring angels to war on my behalf.

Jezebel you are not a queen. You are a witch. You are not a virgin. You are a whore. Every altar of witchcraft and idolatry is being destroyed now. You no longer rule my life.

In Jesus name I now detached the Jezebel spirit from operating in my life, ministry, church, business and marriage. I break the curse of Jezebel back to ten generations on both sides of the family. I cut, sever, break and destroy all cords, snares, fetters, chains and weapons of control and used by this evil network.

All spirits tied to Jezebel, including manipulation, control, Queen of Heaven, Queen of Babylon, hatred of men, anger towards father, rebellion towards husband, male authority, God, the untamed tongue, temper, destruction of the family, women liberation spirits have no power over me.

I rebuke and cut off the harlots and mistresses of Jezebel and break their power my marriage.

I rebuke the spirit of Herodias and break every form of retaliation against my family, my ministry and me.

I rebuke the spirits of witchcraft, lust, seduction, intimidation, idolatry, and whoredom connected to Jezebel.

I war against Jezebel's intimidation and control and boldly declare that every chain that this spirit has been destroyed and broken.

I command Jezebel to be thrown down by her eunuchs' and devoured by the dogs.

I break the power, manipulation, lies, denial, and deception caused by the spirit of Jezebel.

I rebuke all spirits of false teaching & false prophecy connected to Jezebel.

I break the powers of every word curse and witchcraft spoken against my life by Jezebel.

I loose myself from all curses of Jezebel and spirits of Jezebel operating in my bloodline. I break every curse associated with being in Jezebels bedchamber including discouragement, death, humiliation, nakedness, slavery, senility, homosexuality and lesbianism, cancer, schizophrenia, divorce, female domination, male domination, incest, loss of children, loss of spouse, disasters, accidents, loneliness, desolation and financial ruin.

Prayers against Ahab

Father, forgive me for being an enabler to Jezebel by hosting the spirit of Ahab. I repent from all wicked actions and behavior.

I resist and disconnect myself from the spirit of Ahab, Nimrod and Baal.

I renounce my association with passivity, laziness and the spirit of lethargy.

I renounce hatred of women, mother, wife, the fear of women, childishness, cowardice, hidden anger, sluggard, self-hatred, rejection, confusion, perversion, inferiority, jealousy, pride, depression and idolatry.

Basic Deliverance Prayers

I command all generational curses operating in my life to be cast out in the name of Jesus. All pride, rebellion, lust, poverty, witchcraft, idolatry, death, destruction, failure, sickness, infirmity, disease, fear, schizophrenia, double-mindedness and rejection come out now in the name of Jesus.

I command all spirits of lust, perversion, adultery, fornication, masturbation, pornography, uncleanness, homosexuality, bisexuality and immorality to come out of my body, my mind, my will and my emotions in the name of Jesus.

I command all spirits of hurt, hatred, rejection, fear, anger, wrath, sadness, depression, discouragement, grief, bitterness, and un-forgiveness to come out of my emotions in the name of Jesus.

I command all spirits of confusion, forgetfulness, mind control, mental illness, and double mindedness, fantasy, pain, pride and memory recall, to come out of my mind in the name of Jesus.

I command all spirits of guilt, shame, and condemnation to come out of my conscience in the name of Jesus.

I command all spirits of pride, stubbornness, disobedience, rebellion, self-will, selfishness, and arrogance to come out of my will in the name of Jesus.

I command all spirits of witchcraft, sorcery, divination and occult to come out in the name of Jesus.

I command all religious, traditional and racists' spirits to come out in the name of Jesus.

I command spirits of doubt, unbelief, error, heresy, legalism, witchcraft, hatred and murder that came in through religion to come out in the name of Jesus.

I command all spirits of division, discord, racism, pride and perversion that came in through denominations to come out in Jesus name.

I command all evil spirits to detach and come out of my Skeletal system, Digestive system, Muscular system, Lymphatic system, Endocrine system, Nervous system, Cardiovascular system, Reproductive system and Urinary system in Jesus name.

I command all spirits of addiction to come out of my appetite in the name of Jesus.

I command all spirits lodged in my head, eyes, mouth, tongue, ears and throat to come out in the name of Jesus.

I command all spirits lodged in my chest, lungs and esophagus to come out in the name of Jesus.

I command all spirits nested in my back, spine and neck to come out in the name of Jesus.

I command all spirits operating in my stomach, navel, and abdomen to come out in the name of Jesus.

I command all spirits lodged in my heart, spleen, kidneys, liver, gall bladder, intestines and pancreas to come out in the name of Jesus.

I command all spirits operating in my sex organs to come out in the name of Jesus.

I command all spirits operating in my hands, fingers, arms, legs and feet to come out in the name of Jesus.

I command all spirits operating in my glands and lymph nodes to come out in the name of Jesus.

I command all spirits flowing through my blood, arteries, veins and bone marrow to come out in the name of Jesus.

I command all evil spirits attacking my cells to come out in the name of Jesus.

Made in the USA
San Bernardino, CA
27 October 2017